What People Are Saying About
From Heartache to Healing:

A Bishop Sees Hope

I read the Introduction today on the train. This is a message for those looking to put the jigsaw pieces of their lives back together again. Your thoughts and concepts bring hope and faith and a reason to believe that life can be sweet and good again. — Bishop S.

This has Blessed Me as a Future Husband

I'm having a hard time putting into words what your book has meant to me personally and to my fiancée. She and I have had many, many discussions on this topic over our three year courtship. I can't help but feel your words confirming to my heart the issues she has tried to communicate to me, but I just didn't understand until I received a second and third witness from the two of you. I feel like shouting "Hallelujah" as I read and know that some of my fiancée's most tender and deep feelings are finally being addressed. — D.D.

I Wish I'd Had This Book Years Ago!

Fifteen years ago, I made the painful decision to divorce my husband due to pornography addiction and the accompanying abusive behaviors. It was a difficult process and I didn't make that decision lightly. I wish I'd had the concepts in this book to help be back then. I'm definitely giving this book to a dear friend who now finds herself where I was so many years ago. — G.R.

Other titles by Colleen C. Harrison

He Did Deliver Me from Bondage

A Voice from the Fire

Patterns of Light: Step 1

Patterns of Light: Step 2

Patterns of Light: Step 3

Patterns of Light: Steps 4 & 5

Patterns of Light: Step 6

Other titles by Philip A. Harrison

Clean Hands, Pure Heart

Dear Bishop

From Heartache to Healing

Finding Power in Christ to Deal with a Loved One's Sexual Addiction

Colleen C. Harrison

Philip A. Harrison

Windhaven Publishing
12 Step Materials for the LDS Community
HYRUM, UTAH

PO BOX 31
HYRUM, UT 84319
WWW.WINDHAVENPUBLISHING.COM

Copyright © 2010 Colleen C. Harrison, Philip A. Harrison
        and Windhaven Recovery, Inc. dba Windhaven Publishing and Productions
Printed in the United States of America

ISBN: 978-1-930738-21-8

13 12 11 10 9 8 7 6 5 4 3 2 1

The Twelve Steps and Twelve Traditions have been reprinted and adapted with permission from Alcoholics Anonymous World Services, Inc. The opinions expressed are not to be attributed to Alcoholics Anonymous. Information from various Heart t' Heart printed materials has been reprinted and adapted with permission from the General Service Board of Heart t' Heart, Inc.

Quotes from Alcoholics Anonymous (the "Big Book") are taken from the 4th Edition.

Cover Art: "Touch of Faith," © Simon Dewey. Used with permission. Courtesy Altus Fine Arts.
Cover Design: Bryan Crockett.
Interior Design & Typesetting: LibrisPro, Pleasant Grove, Utah.

This book is designed to provide you with information on Twelve Step recovery so that you can deal more effectively with compulsive/addictive behaviors in yourself or in those you love. However, results from applying these principles will vary with the individual. As a result, this book is sold with the understanding that neither the author nor the publisher is engaged in rendering specific psychotherapy or other professional counseling services to any individual.

ACKNOWLEDGMENTS

We have so much to be grateful for in the production of this book. Most of all, first and last we are indebted to the Lord for the ideas and concepts that have changed our lives and that have led us to know Him as the most important partner in our marriage and in every aspect of our lives.

We'd like to thank Him for the following people who we recognize as His instruments in helping us bring this book into being. We'll try to list you in order according to the stages of the book's development.

Susan, Joy, Julie Ann, and Karlene who were our cheerleading squad from the beginning, telling us over and over that we could do this. You'll all be mentioned again since you midwifed this book right through to the final delivery. (We know we're mixing our metaphors, but you got to understand we're nearly hysterical with joy to finally be done!)

For Susan and David Edwards: Thanks so much Suzie and David for letting Colleen "retreat" to your home for several weeks so she could give her full attention to this manuscript.

For Joy S. Thanks Joy for sponsoring me (Colleen) through over twenty years of recovery and listening to "it all"—my joys and my rants. And thanks for sitting with me through the close read and copy editing on every chapter of this book. Your voice is scattered throughout and increases its readability many fold.

To Peg W. for reading through early drafts with us, helping us catch glitches and cheering us on. Peg, we are so grateful for your sweet sisterhood and the blessing of having a home-away-from-home with you when we're in Salt Lake City.

Thanks to Jody and Delmy and all the other Heart t' Heart sisters (and brothers) who have read early drafts and given us such great feedback, and also to those dear sisters whose testimonies we were blessed to scatter through the chapters.

To Karlene Browning for her expertise in the small-press publishing business and with typesetting. We can't tell you, Karlene, how grateful we are that you have such a perfect blend of talent and skill for this. Without you, we'd be turning to strangers and that would be a sadness we hope to never have to deal with.

To Bryan Crockett for all the help on last minute cover design.

To the power-people behind the scenes that make a book come true: Valerie Brough for her miraculous ability to copy edit with exquisite thoroughness; Bryan Crockett and Book Printers of Utah who has always done the most professional job for us on any book; Barry Reader and Brigham Distributing, who does such a great job of helping us get books to retailers.

And finally, to our children for their patience in having parents who have chosen to be as disclosing and candid as we've felt the Lord has called us to be in bearing testimony of the Lord's goodness in blessing us with recovery.

TABLE OF CONTENTS

Section 1: Discovering the Truth, Confronting the Lies

Section 2: Continuing in the Truth, Outliving the Lies

A Personal Introduction

Colleen's Story

When I joined the LDS church at age fourteen, the single doctrine that attracted me more than any other was that of eternal marriage. When I married five years later, I was determined to dedicate my life to this doctrine, to sacrifice anything to make sure my marriage lasted forever. Over the next twenty-three years, I poured my heart and soul into being the most active LDS woman I could imagine. I attended every meeting, held every position I was called to, gave birth to as many children as I could (twelve), and tried to understand why, no matter what I did, my husband was never satisfied with me—sexually or in any other way. Instead of feeling joyful and fulfilled, I spent my life in a nearly constant state of confusion and discouragement, wondering what was wrong with me.

Totally unbeknownst to me, my husband was practicing a sexual addiction that he had been indulging in since he was a teen. At no point in his life had he ever been concerned enough about his behaviors to tell anyone about them. All along he believed Satan, the father of lies, who convinced him that his choices weren't really "that bad," and that keeping them a secret would never fail him, that his secret indulgences could go on indefinitely even while he was performing publically as a faithful LDS man. Gradually, just as the scriptures warn, his conscience seared **"with a hot iron,"**[1] he rationalized and justified involving his own child in his lust.

Meanwhile, I was so distracted by trying to hide the continual spirit of blame and contention that permeated our private family life that I was oblivious to his hideous secret. I was blinded by the belief that since

I, as mother, was supposed to be the heart of my home, all of our problems in the home and family must be due to my failure. Surely, if I just did more, did better, was a better wife and mother, the Spirit of the Lord would be with us more.

Then one day, the truth about the depths of my husband's descent into evil came out, as my precious daughter disclosed to me his sexual behaviors toward her. While I have heard of wives who have been able and willing to face this level of heartache and go on with their marriage, I honestly could not feel the Lord asking that of me. Though it took several years to convince me that I had to leave my husband to the rescue of the only One who could save him, I did eventually accept that what I felt was, without a shadow of a doubt, an "honorable release" from the marriage. I felt the Lord's testimony that I had done all that I could do and my offering was acceptable to Him, that it was enough.

Like Lehi, I felt God's witness of truth to my heart that it was time to leave all that was secure and familiar behind.[2] I needed to take my children with me and trust that the Lord would lead us as we faced the equivalent of a journey into an unknown wilderness. Paradoxically, I was strengthened by the Lord's own spirit, as I did what I knew had to be done. I ended the marriage. I knew that no matter what lay ahead, nothing could be more harmful to my children than my husband's refusal to own his actions with a broken heart and contrite spirit. Thus I learned first-hand the devastating truth that there are times when divorce, with all its challenges, is the "lesser of two evils."

So it was that in June, 1991, I became a single parent with eight children between the ages of six and seventeen still to raise. I was alone, and yet, I did not feel as alone and vulnerable as I had in my marriage. I felt the Lord cleaving to me, keeping me safe in His Spirit, and with all the desperation of a drowning person, I clung to Him. Though my testimony of Him felt still and small at times, it never left me. Fortunately for me, I had already been studying and practicing the Twelve Steps during the previous ten years in order to maintain some degree of recovery from my own tendency to use food as an addiction. I knew what it meant to rely on the Lord to do for me what I had no idea how to do for myself. He would not fail me. I had to trust that He would lead me one day and one step at a time. Still, it was obvious that I would need to do something to support myself and my children. Upheld by His Spirit, I resolutely turned my face toward the future and began to look at my options for work or schooling. I prayed that the Lord would light my way into whatever path He knew was best for me.

One of my options was to immediately find a job, but what kind of job? I was a teen in the 1960s, when Church leaders counseled young women not to put anything, even education, ahead of marriage. I married after only one year of college. I had been a stay-at-home mom for twenty-three years. What skills or qualifications could I put on an employment application? This reality pointed me toward the other option of returning to school to pursue a degree that would afford me far more earning potential. The thought of re-entering the world of books and tests and grades was overwhelming, but I felt the Spirit of the Lord leading me. It made no sense, but I felt a warm, glowing, peaceful excitement. Other options left me cold, feeling shut down and bothered.

For the next five years, supported by various forms of financial aid, I attended Brigham Young University and eventually graduated with a MA in English with an emphasis in journal and memoir writing. During those same years, I pursued and completed the course work for certification as an addictions counselor through the University of Utah and finished writing the book, *He Did Deliver Me from Bondage*. After a brief post-graduation pause for further consultation with the Lord, I applied and was accepted into a doctoral program in Family and Human Development at Utah State University in Logan, Utah.

Again, I was faced with stepping off into the unknown as I prepared to relocate myself and my two youngest children—the only ones still living with me. As I drove away from the house my husband and I had moved into fourteen years earlier, a house that I had thought we would grow old in, a house that I thought would be the place our children and grandchildren would love to come home to, I could truly identify with the feelings of the early pioneers. I set my face toward a life that had turned into exactly the opposite of what I had expected.

I spent the next two years in Logan, sharing a house with my married daughter, attending school full-time and teaching undergraduate classes part-time. Once again, I thought I knew what the Lord wanted of me. I pictured that I would finish raising my youngest children, complete my PhD, and go on to teach and hopefully do more writing. However, in the summer of 1998, I learned that the Lord had an even greater education in mind for me when he moved me to Cache Valley. He was going to help me heal from the devastation of my first marriage to a sexually addicted partner, ironically enough, by inviting me to marry another sexually addicted man. He wanted me to learn what only a repentant man could teach me—a man's sexual addiction is not about his wife's inadequacy.

Though Phil had also struggled with his addiction since his teens, unlike my first husband, he had never justified it or pretended to himself it was okay. Instead, he had repeatedly sought out priesthood leaders to confess his problem and to reach out for help. Neither did he blame his wife for his behaviors. He was humble and honest about his weakness. He was willing to admit it was an addiction and to do all that he could to participate in his own recovery. In the first year we were married, I watched him slip several times, but he never tried to minimize or hide it. Every time he slipped, I would turn to the Lord, seeking His counsel and comfort, and every time, I would feel His love for Phil. I would feel His testimony that Phil's heart was in the right place—turned to Him— and that I could trust that Phil's desire to be clean was genuine and would eventually mature into complete and lasting recovery.

The Lord's promise was finally realized. Phil's slips became fewer and further between. As of this writing, he is rejoicing in over ten years of deliverance from his addiction. I have watched a miracle. My trust and faith in God's ability to change lives and restore a person to complete wholeness has been affirmed. I am filled with wonder and awe at His mercy and grace every time I observe Phil's healed soul. He is as innocent and without guile as a little child and yet so wise because of his experience. His testimony of the Savior's Atonement is unwavering and powerful, and blesses the lives of others.

Today, I enjoy the safety and oneness of a marriage between two partners who are both grounded firmly on faith in the Lord Jesus Christ, not faith in each other. The Savior is the heart of our home and in Him we have **"a perfect brightness of hope"**[3] for ourselves and for our marriage. We pray continually to be able to convey this voice of hope to you, to strengthen you in your own journey from heartache to healing.

A Little of Phil's Story

How grateful I am to be able to share with you the miracle that has happened in my life and to share the hope I have for you and your husband. I also must thank Colleen for her kind words.

About six months before my first wife, Kathy, suffered heart failure and passed away, she and I found Heart t' Heart and quickly became close friends with Colleen. Like Colleen, Kathy had been involved in Twelve Step programs and so I knew something about the steps through her. Still, I had never tried to apply them to myself.

It wasn't until I started to learn the LDS version of the steps that I began to realize that I was, in fact, an addict. This was a hard thing to face, but in doing so, something else began to happen that helped me to stand still and not deny the truth of it. I started to come to know my Savior for the first time. This sounds strange to write, because I was an active Latter-day Saint all my life. I thought I knew a lot about the Savior. I discovered, though, that knowing about Him wasn't the same thing as knowing Him. For example, I couldn't imagine that the Lord wasn't as disgusted with me about my addiction as I was with myself. I blamed and shamed myself and thought He was inspiring me to do that. When I really came to know Him, I found that He felt exactly the opposite about me. I felt His Spirit testifying to me that He had never stopped loving me or having faith in me! I felt that He had been waiting, all along, for me to come to Him with the reality of how powerless I was to save myself. When I did, He received me with open arms.

One of the beliefs I held in the past that kept me from coming directly to the Lord was that I had to prove myself "worthy" before I sought Him. Only then could I expect Him to help me. As I studied the true principles in the Twelve Steps, using *He Did Deliver Me from Bondage* as a study guide to the Book of Mormon, I began to realize that by holding this belief, I was reversing the order of true repentance.

For the first time in my life, I actually heard Moroni's testimony: **"Yea, come unto Christ, and be perfected in him, and deny yourselves of all ungodliness..."**[4] and saw that the first thing I needed to do, even while I was still unworthy, was to come unto Christ. Why? Because only in Him would I find the power to deny myself of the ungodliness of my pornography addiction. It was only when I came to the Savior just as I was, in the middle of my messed up life, and admitted that I couldn't get rid of this addiction without His help, that things started to change.

Citing **Doctrine and Covenants 6:36** in which the Lord testifies, **"Look unto me in every thought,"** the text of *He Did Deliver Me from Bondage* helped me see that I could actually turn to the Lord even in the moment of my worst temptations, not just in my righteous thoughts. As that testimony sunk into my heart, I came to the place where I could humbly turn to Him right in the moment, and say, "Lord, I can't handle this temptation, please take it away." And He would.

Even more miraculously, I found that He never became impatient with me, even when I had to cry out to Him in my heart many times in the same day, sometimes in the same hour. Every time I did, I found His power with me, sustaining me. Thus, in His power, not mine, I found myself able to remain abstinent, one day at a time. Those single days have now added up to many amazing years of deliverance from a sin that I thought would destroy my life. The thing I must always testify of and never forget, though, is that it is *His* strength that is working this miracle in my life, not my own. For over thirty years, I couldn't put together more than a few weeks of abstinence, and without Him, I can't do it now, either. But Christ can, and He does.

What is my part? What do I have to do? I have to be willing to put my relationship with Him first, above all other relationships. Although my recovery grows stronger with the passing years, I know I must remain watchful. Even more importantly, I need to always remember where the power came from that enabled me to become abstinent in the first place. I must acknowledge that power as it continues to support me from day to day. I have to stay in close touch with Him every day, but that has only convinced me how much He loves me—and I know He loves each of you that much, too, and will help you to find your way through the confusion and pain you are now feeling.

That is the message I hope to support Colleen in sharing with you—that there is a way out of this hell, for both you and your husband. The Savior can change lives. He can lift us from these awful depths and give us a life of peace and happiness, free from the anguish that years of addiction have inevitably caused. In the years since Kathy's passing and my marriage to Colleen, I have been blessed to share my experience of coming to know and apply the Savior's atoning power in detail in my book, *Clean Hands, Pure Heart: Overcoming Addiction to Pornography Through the Redeeming Power of Jesus Christ.*

Now, it is my blessing and privilege to join Colleen in sharing the message of this book, *From Heartache to Healing.* I hope that it will be a blessing to you to hear some of the thoughts I can contribute as a recovering husband and father. Let me begin by assuring you that the Lord loves you and wants to help you find peace, right now, right where you are, whether your husband chooses to change or not.

Colleen has learned how to support a husband in his recovery while not interfering with his agency and accountability before the Lord. She has inspired and blessed me with her example since the first day she agreed to marry me. Still, in and through the ten years we've been together, she has left me alone to work out my recovery with the Lord. She has taught me that my wife can't save me, any more than I can save myself. She has modeled for me what it looks like and feels like to go to the Savior for the hope and strength it takes to face life's hard times without resorting to addictive behavior.

I thank the Lord continually for her willingness to believe in me and to believe in Christ even more. The tragic loss of Colleen's first marriage to sexual addiction stands in stark contrast to the healing of our lives and the joy we feel as we both come to Christ and experience the sealing bond of His Spirit. Because she has lived through both circumstances, I believe she has a unique ability to empathize with other sisters, no matter which direction their husbands may choose to take.

You and your husband are both experiencing one of the most challenging scourges of our times. But there are principles that will help. Most importantly, the Savior is there for you. He has blessed my life and Colleen's life, and we know He will bless yours as well. Thank you for letting us be part of your journey.

Our United Testimony

You need to know up front that we both believe that there can be no heart-deep, genuine healing for a Latter-day Saint woman (or man) if her efforts at recovery do not center on and arise out of the words of Christ perceived and believed in the private, personal, sacred places of her own heart. It is our testimony that no amount of talk therapy, guided imagery, or emotional release work, and no number of books read, priesthood leaders counseled with, or loved ones gathered round to support you, will bring you the heart-deep, soul-satisfying comfort and counsel that the Lord's own testimony will bring to you.

We hope to share enough of our experience, faith and hope in Christ in the pages of this book that you can feel His presence in your own heart and mind as you read. We pray that you will not only read and say, "I recognize this story. It is so much like mine," but that you will continue to read and begin to say, "I believe their testimony. I feel a hope in Christ awakening and strengthening in my heart."

We offer this testimony that we have lived in the name of Jesus Christ, Amen.

1. 1 Timothy 4:2

2. 1 Nephi 2:1-3.

3. 2 Nephi 31:20.

4. Moroni 10:32.

Behold, the LORD hath proclaimed
unto the end of the world,
Say ye to the daughter of Zion,
Behold, thy salvation cometh.

— Isaiah 62:11

Section 1

Discovering the Truth, Confronting the Lies

Chapter **1**

Where to Start?

The usual place to start is with an introduction, so let's do that first.

Hi, Colleen and Phil here! If we could welcome you into our home and sit down with you one-on-one, we'd be delighted to do so, but since time and expense prohibit that, we are trusting the testimony of the Lord to our hearts that it will be just as good—maybe even better—to put our sharing in writing and send it out to each of you via this book.

Who are we? What are our credentials? How can we presume to offer you help with what you're facing? In one sentence: we are survivors of the heart-breaking experience of sexual addiction and its consequences on family members. Phil struggled with pornography addiction from the time he was a teen, but has been in recovery and clean from his sexual addiction since November 1999. My first husband refused to deal with his sexual addiction. I was forced to face and recover from a codependent relationship with him and end our marriage of twenty-three years in 1991. I have also had to learn how to allow the Lord to sustain me through many heart-rending moments in my children's lives as they, too, have fallen prey to various addictions.

To Wives and Other Loved Ones

We are well aware that there are husbands with sexually addicted wives, as well as parents and others with sexually addicted loved ones, who long to find literature addressing their situations. Nevertheless, we have followed the persistent impression to direct our thoughts to the wives and fiancées of men who struggle with sexual addiction.

If you are a husband or loved one of a sexually addicted person, we pray that the Spirit of the Lord will guide you to adapt and apply the ideas in *From Heartache to Healing* to your individual needs. Virtually all recovery literature based on the Twelve Steps contains true principles from which every addict and every loved one of an addict can benefit.

Colleen: Sharing with Each of You as Individuals

Phil and I speak to each of you as friends and fellow survivors in this battle Satan is waging against the Saints. Neither of us pretends to represent the voice of secular education and professional counseling, helpful as that voice may be. We believe the contributions of science can give addicts and family members great techniques and much thoughtful advice based on the latest studies and theories. We have both been through PhD programs and trained in the scientific method. While all of that learning was good, it did not reach to the depths of the human soul where the testimony of living experience can reach.

We know by our own experience that there is a very special kind of help that can only be found when personal experience, shared feelings, and living testimony speak heart to heart. Thus, Phil and I will be drawing primarily upon our own experiences as a man and wife who have faced and survived the ravages of sexual addiction. Besides the "authority" of our own experience, we will be relying wholly upon the counsel of the prophets of the Lord, and through their testimonies, of the Lord Himself.

As you read, you will find that some sections are written in our united voice while other sections will be designated as either one or the other of us, just as this section is in my voice. We have done this because as we sit at our desks typing these thoughts, we are wishing we could be with each of you in person. Thus it is our desire that the voice in these pages will feel to you like we are sitting across from you in our living room rather than speaking to you from a podium or pulpit.

We invite you to use your imagination and visualize each of these chapters as if it were a separate conversation with us. Granted, we will be doing most of the initial "talking" in print as you read our words, but we encourage you to respond the same way—in print. We encourage you to get up right now and find pen and paper—journal or notebook— where you can jot down your thoughts as they come in response to our thoughts. We hope you will use this technique throughout *From Heartache to Healing* so that your reading experience can be as close to a dialogue between us as possible. We also welcome your direct responses and feedback at the following e-mail or post office address:

FHTH@windhavenpublishing.com

Windhaven Publishing, P.O. Box 31, Hyrum, UT 84319

We would love to hear from you and will do our best to answer each of you personally.

In Their Own Voices

Included in the following chapters you will also "hear" the sharing of other LDS women who are dealing with their husbands' sexual addictions. These comments and testimonies were originally posted anonymously on an online spouses' support forum. Out of gratitude for these sisters courageous sharing and with a desire to help their voices reach as many readers as possible, we have included excerpts woven throughout the book. For the sake of anonymity we have used pseudonyms and eliminated personal details.

We know that you will be blessed by their long-distance fellowship and hope that you may be encouraged to participate in such a support system yourself. (See Appendix for a list of online forums.) These forums can be a great help if you are concerned about keeping yourself strictly anonymous or if you do not have a local LDS support group to attend.

The Repetition of Certain Themes in This Book

As we address the different issues in each chapter, you will find several major themes or testimonies repeated over and over, such as:

- Your husband's addiction is not a reflection of anything about you.

- You are not responsible for his recovery, only for your own.

- You and your husband are not each other's worst enemies—no matter how much you may feel that way at this point. Satan is the enemy of you both.

- You and your husband can find hope and recovery from the wounds Satan has inflicted upon you as you follow the principles in the LDS version of the Twelve Steps.

- The twelve true principles found in the Twelve Steps will lead you along a pathway of honesty and humility that will bring you closer to Heavenly Father and the Savior than you may have ever imagined possible.

- You *can* survive this! You *can* heal from this! You *can* outlive this experience. There can *and will* be life after this. We offer our stories and our lives as living proof of that testimony. Someday, this season of terrible heartache and confusion will be behind you; it will be history.

Though it may feel totally insane to consider these ideas from where you are today—with your dreams shattered around you. However, we know you can emerge from this experience far more mature, more compassionate, more patient, and with greater capacity for love, and yes, even joy, than you have ever known. We speak to you from that place of recovery in our own lives. We readily admit that it feels almost like a form of resurrection, of having been returned to life. We know the reality of the Savior's power in our lives.

We pray that you may feel our love for Him and for you throughout this book. We pray that reading this book will bless you with an increase in your sense of His love for you so that you can trust Him even in the otherwise overwhelming challenges you face. We pray that your ability to feel His peace will increase while you read this book. There is no one and nowhere else you can turn that can give you the peace that only the Savior Himself can administer. The peace He gives is a **"peace...which passeth all understanding."**[1] We will be coming back to this theme many times throughout the following chapters. This is the only peace that can enter into the depths of your heart and create a haven for His Spirit, so that He can sustain you through the storm and walk with you across the crashing waves created by sexual addiction in these last days.

Starting Where *You* Are

If we could meet with you face-to-face, the next thing we'd want to know is where you are right now along the path of discovering your loved one's sexual addiction and dealing with it. We'd invite you to share some of your story with us. We'd probably ask a few questions like:

- How long have you known about your husband's addiction? Did you just learn about it or have you been struggling with knowledge of it for years?

- Have you had a chance to do much research on the subject of sexual addiction or are you still in shock at having to even use those words?

- Is this book your first effort to reach out for help?

- What other books have you read?

- Have you been trying to deal with this all alone or have you talked with anyone else yet? With your bishop, a parent, a family member, a best friend?

- Are you seeking or have you found a professional marriage and family therapist who understands addiction and respects your religious beliefs? Does he or she know about the growing number of resources available in the LDS community?

- Do you feel like you're on the verge of a separation? Maybe even a divorce?

By asking those questions, we would be doing a sort of triage assessment of the nature of your individual wounds and which order of response we could make that would be tailored directly to your personal needs. Since we can't do that, we'd like to suggest that you turn back to the Table of Contents at the front of this book and read through the chapter titles and subtitles prayerfully. Ask Heavenly Father to highlight for you those chapters and sections of chapters that He knows would address your most pressing needs. It may be to start at the very beginning with just what "addiction" is and what the prophets have said about it. If this is the case, then reading Chapter Two, "What It Means to Be Addicted," would be the place to start. If, however, your heart is breaking over questions like, "What did I do to deserve this?" or "What do I do now to control his acting out?" then you'll see in the Table of Contents that other chapters may be the place to turn first.

Whether you need to do some quick first-aid reading of specific chapters after this one, or you feel able to settle in and read straight through the chapters in order, we do recommend that you read all of Section One, "Discovering the Truth, Confronting the Lies," before moving on to Section Two, "Continuing in the Truth, Outliving the Lies," and all of Section Two before moving on to Section Three, "Embracing Your Common Need for Recovery." This will give you the best foundation to build upon as you move forward.

Our prayers and blessings go with you.

---

1. Philippians 4:7.

2 *What It Means To Be Addicted*

We understand how tempting it is to want to believe your husband's behavior is just a very disgusting and ugly bad habit. We know you want to believe that if you could just convince him how disgusting and hurtful it is, he'd come to his senses, put it down, scrub his mind with a wire brush and be done with it.

You might be surprised to know that those are exactly the same thoughts he had about his involvement in pornography when he started. When he was first exposed to it and didn't turn away, you can be sure he assumed that he'd eventually just make up his mind, exercise a little willpower (okay, a *lot* of willpower), and be done with it. But when he finally tried, he found he couldn't stop, at least not permanently. In this chapter we hope to help increase your understanding of why your husband can't just stop, even though he may want to with the same desperation a drowning man feels to breathe.

Why? Because a bad habit is to an addiction what a mosquito bite is to a shark bite. What a skinned knee is to leprosy. What a tonsillectomy is to a heart transplant. What the common cold is to the black plague.

We believe the following is a good working definition of addiction and conveys the whole truth about its scope and power:

> Addiction exists when the repeated use of a mood-altering substance or behavior results in a person

becoming so dependent on the substance or behavior that they can find no way to permanently stop, even when continuing the behavior is causing serious damage to their relationships, health, employment, and personal sense of serenity and spirituality.

The Enemy Has Infiltrated Our Ranks

In the LDS community, most of us have believed that if we would avoid the use of addictive *substances*, we could ignore the whole subject of addiction. We have been oblivious to the reality that Satan has infiltrated our lives and is mounting an all-out war by luring us into behaviors that can be every bit as devastating as a Word of Wisdom problem.

The fact is that any activity that offers a person even a temporary escape from stress or other challenging feelings can become an addiction. Whatever *it* is, we almost always start out thinking we'll indulge "just this once." Thus, abuse of prescription drugs, gambling, excessive spending, excessive use of television and other forms of electronic media such as computers, electronic games, and fantasy games, are some of the most prevalent addictive behaviors today. In the LDS culture just as in the world in general, unhealthy eating behaviors are rapidly becoming more than just bad habits for many who find that no number of diets, exercise programs, or weight-loss drugs can provide them with permanent relief. Just one more bite, one more brownie, one more meal—then we'll "go on the wagon."

As challenging as it may be for us as members of a church culture whose very identity is founded on "Deseret" (the honey bee and the continuous busyness of the beehive), we are having to recognize that it can become an addiction to be compulsively working, serving others, reading, exercising, cleaning our homes and many other good things found on the ideal "to do" list.

Why? Because all of these behaviors—even living as perfectly as possible, checking an ever increasing number of "should's" and "have-to's" off a list—can be motivated by the need to distract ourselves from fear, anxiety, sorrow, regret, guilt, shame, and resentment, just to name a few of the negative feelings mortality presents us with.

These behaviors have the ability to mask and postpone negative feelings by triggering rushes of adrenaline, dopamine and other mood-altering chemicals. Thus, when we indulge in any of these activities excessively, we must prayerfully ask this question: *Am I doing this because it brings me joy and peace, or because I am feeling compelled to do it?*

If, in all honesty, we have to admit we are doing these things to avoid negative feelings, we need to face the fact we are practicing an addiction.

Still, even in the face of how widespread addictive behaviors can be, there is no other addiction among the Saints that is taking a greater toll in terms of devastated lives and disrupted families than addiction to pornography. As President Ezra Taft Benson declared:

> **The plaguing sin of this generation is sexual immorality. This, the Prophet Joseph said, would be the source of more temptations, more buffetings, and more difficulties for the elders of Israel than any other (see *Journal of Discourses*, 8:55) (President Ezra Taft Benson, "Cleansing the Inner Vessel," *Ensign*, May 1986, 4).**

Satan not only desires your husband's downfall. He desires the downfall of you, your children, and your children's children, as well. With this understanding, it can provide some comfort to know that the prophets of God have foreseen the battle in which we find ourselves immersed. It is further testimony that we do have a Father in Heaven who is aware of our burden. We can be sure He has prepared a way for us to rise triumphant from even a blow as devastating as addiction.

Let us say it again, as gently but as firmly as we can: *Your husband can't stop using pornography on his own, no matter how much he loves you, or how much love you extend to him, or how much pressure you put on him.*

The truth is, without realizing it, he has wandered down a progressive path into Satan's single most powerful trap—addiction. Nothing you do is going to save him. The only thing you can do to help him, or to help any person who is struggling with an addiction, is to set the example of coming to Christ for your own sake.

What Makes Pornography Addiction So Powerful?

Traditionally, those who work with drug and alcohol abuse define addiction as taking a foreign substance into the body frequently enough that the body adjusts to its presence and goes through severe symptoms of withdrawal when deprived of it. Admittedly, people who attempt to quit a behavioral addiction may not experience the kind of physical pain, cold sweats, and *delirium tremens* suffered by someone coming off hard drugs or alcohol. This can invite the deceptive impression that those with behavioral addictions don't really suffer from dependency and withdrawal. The reality is quite the opposite.

Those who have become addicted to the sexual arousal stimulated by viewing pornography relate very closely with the behaviors, emotions and thinking of people addicted to substances like drugs or alcohol. In fact, Elder Dallin H. Oaks quoted one brother who testified that "quitting even the hardest drugs was nothing" in comparison to trying to quit sexual addiction.[1]

There's a very logical reason for this reality. Of all the behaviors that could become addictive, there are none that alter the body's internal chemistry more powerfully than sexual arousal. One bishop referred to this physical change as "arousal on demand" (see Elder Oak's talk cited above). Even though these chemicals are produced by the body instead of being introduced through a pill or needle, they are no less real. Thus, the use of pornography is definitely a "mood-altering" experience that can be almost immediately addictive.

Phil: Can a Person Really Lose Their Agency?

Nobody starts viewing pornography in the hope of becoming addicted. In our day and age, a young man's first exposure to pornography is very likely not a deliberate choice of his own. Nowadays, becoming exposed to pornographic images is not really a question of "if" but "when." A person can hardly turn on any commercial television channel or stand in line at a grocery store without being exposed.

Fortunately, many men are able to turn away from such inadvertent exposure. On the other hand, many other men and virtually all boys are enticed to take a second look. Then, when they realize that a little curious looking has become a compulsion—something they feel compelled to do again, even though they really meant to give it up—they are already deep into the adversary's snare. Many pornography addicts have truly tried to quit over and over again, even before anyone else found out what they were doing. They may have tried dozens of times, but found they could not stay away. Trying to hide their panic, even from themselves, they begin to despair. The irrational result? They often give up trying to quit all together.

I can testify how it feels to get lost in the darkness of repeated surrender to temptation. By giving in over and over, the reaction becomes so ingrained that eventually there is no thought, no decision, no attempt to resist the urge. There is just a following of the temptation, wherever the tempter chooses to lead, as if one were in a trance. It's as if there is no choice but to give in. The temptations seem overwhelming, and the will to resist seems to have disappeared somewhere along the way. That is why so many addicts come to a place of feeling hopeless about ever getting well. Like me, they have tried over and over to break free, only to find their own strength woefully insufficient. After repeatedly trying and failing, I came to the point where I thought recovery was impossible and began to respond like a total slave. I had become convinced that I was lost, doomed to unending bondage to the enemy of my soul.

Paradoxically, one reason Satan has been able to virtually sneak up and establish such a battle-front right in our midst is because of our belief that we are free agents and will always be able to make a right choice if we want to badly enough. What we haven't realized is that while we are all born with our agency intact, we can have experiences after coming into mortality that compromise or cause us to forfeit our ability to choose for ourselves "almost to the vanishing point," according to President Marion G. Romney.

> The free agency possessed by any one person is increased or diminished by the use to which he puts it. Every wrong decision one makes restricts the area in which he can thereafter exercise his agency. The further one goes in the making of wrong decisions in the exercise of free agency, the more difficult it is for him to recover the lost ground. One can, by persisting long enough, reach the point of no return. He then becomes an abject slave. By the exercise of his free agency, he has decreased the area in which he can act, almost to the vanishing point (Marion G. Romney, "The Perfect Law of Liberty" *Ensign*, Nov. 1981, 43).

Other Apostles and Prophets, such as Elder Russell M. Nelson[2] and Elder Boyd K. Packer[3] have also borne prophetic testimony to the fact that a person can literally lose the ability to exercise their own will by slipping ever so gradually into the severe bondage of addiction.

How Did It Become an Addiction?

Every addiction, not just pornography addiction, begins as one single act against one's conscience. At that moment, when the potential addict goes against the Light of Christ and ignores the truth, that person begins to forfeit their "response-ability," or in other words, their ability to resist the next act. Before they know it, they are repeating the act, and most likely they have begun to do it in secret.

This is how you can tell the difference between a habit and a *bad* habit—when it must be done in secret. Soon, the bad habit has become something the person begins to depend upon. They need it to help them feel able to cope with life. An addiction has formed. Just as the Book of Mormon testifies, Satan's enticements, which began as light as flaxen cords,[4] end up being the very chains and fetters and shackles of hell.[5] As the addiction tightens its grip, the person caught in it begins to care more for the addictive substance or behavior than for anything else in their life. Possession is not too strong a word for the end stage of this downward spiral.

The Loss of Agency to Addiction

Single Act
(done in ignorance or foolish experimentation)

Repeated Act
(sought out deliberately in order to alter mood)

Habit
(return to behavior over and over again—
but is still a matter of choice)

Addiction/Compulsion
(loss of ability to resist doing it—
the addiction takes on a life of its own)

Obsession/Mental Illness/Insanity
(loss of ability to stop thinking about it)

Possession
(loss of all light, destruction of life,
both spiritual and physical)

We hope that seeing the progressive nature of addiction may help you understand that your husband most likely started out as the really decent guy you originally thought him to be, but he has contracted a serious mental/emotional/spiritual illness that cannot be minimized or ignored. The lying spirit of the adversary is at the root of addiction and must be countered with truth. Addiction will only grow worse in the fertile, dark soil of secrecy and denial.

Phil: Accepting the Diagnosis of Addiction

It may be very hard to accept the diagnosis of your husband's problem as an addiction. To use that word makes it sound so serious. But for me, it was a great blessing to identify exactly what I was dealing with. Calling the problem an addiction is no worse than calling diabetes, diabetes. Using the correct term for it is not going to make the reality worse. In fact it's going to set you free to deal with it frankly. It is so important to acknowledge the seriousness of addiction; it's hardly an exaggeration to say it is a matter of life and death. If you resist accepting the reality about his addiction, you won't be willing to go through the steps necessary to help your husband deal with it.

Think of it this way: If you turn your ankle and think it is only sprained, you likely won't go to the doctor. But when the pain continues to get worse, you may start to suspect that your ankle is actually broken and needs a doctor's care. Calling the injury a sprain and treating it as such allows more damage to occur while you continue to walk on an ankle that is truly broken. Once you accept the diagnosis of a break and seek treatment, healing can occur.

My own tendency to minimize my problem kept me from finding real help for years. It is my hope and prayer that in being honest and sharing my own experiences, I can encourage you, as well as your husband, to come out of denial and seek help immediately.

Colleen: Please Seek Help for Yourself

One of the most universal hallmarks of addiction is the desire to keep it a secret. The addict is always reluctant to let anyone know of the problem. Perhaps he has told you of the problem on his own, or maybe you have discovered his secret independently. In any case, you are hurting and need help. You need to talk to someone, even if you don't want to. Secrecy breeds more disease. One must let the light in to allow the healing begin.

My dear sister, I hope you won't mind my reiterating this thought just one more time: *You need to seek help for yourself.* You're hurting. You need to take care of your own mental, emotional, physical, and spiritual health, no matter what your husband does. We'll talk more about that in a later chapter. For now, suffice it to say, one of you has to go for help.

To pretend you can take care of this problem secretly, on your own, just between the two of you, without sacrificing your privacy (pride) is another lie of the devil. He is attempting to keep you in isolation until the disease has destroyed your marriage and family.

Run, don't walk—no matter how bad it hurts—to your nearest priesthood leader, whether your husband agrees or knows. This is not an area where your husband's feelings can righteously interfere with your need for help. If he hasn't yet figured out just how potentially terminal his condition can become, then what you are learning may be the most important truth you can offer him. But first you have to get it, absorb it, believe it—and grab the lifeline of recovery for yourself.

Do You Have a Behavior You Struggle to Control?

As you begin to realize that addiction can come in many forms, you may be able to identify a behavior that you've tried to eliminate from your own life, but without lasting success. This honest realization may help you relate to your husband's dilemma. Please know that we do not suggest this exercise of self-examination in order to detract in any way from the seriousness of your husband's addiction, or to subject you to any more shame or guilt. We suggest it simply as a very profound way that may help you to comprehend how addiction could have such a terrible hold on your husband's life.

Colleen: My Experience with My Own Addictive Behavior

I am absolutely sure that one reason I was able to understand and bear the reality of Phil's addiction was because I was able to empathize with him. I understood what it felt like to be addicted myself.

Since 1981 when I first attended a Twelve Step recovery group focused on unhealthy eating patterns, I had known that, for me, eating was a mood-altering experience—and certain foods were more mood-altering than others. Though I was constantly obsessing about my weight and the latest diet craze, I could not resist the urge to consume unhealthy types and amounts of food any better than an alcoholic could turn down alcohol. My weight increased until I was over 300 pounds! I think we would all have to agree that I was living up to our earlier definition of addiction as "causing serious damage to [my] relationships, health… and personal sense of serenity and spirituality."

In my personal preface to *He Did Deliver Me from Bondage*, I wrote:

> In 1981 I tipped the scale at over 300 pounds. Believe me, I was the most miserable "active" Latter-day Saint I knew. Of course, I didn't know many people, Latter-day Saint or otherwise, because of the isolated, imprisoned lifestyle I lived. I walled myself in with cleaning, cooking, canning, sewing, even with children and husband and, of course, with eating. … Eating was the one thing I consistently did for myself. Mother, the supreme nurturer and caretaker, finally got around to nurturing and taking care of herself at midnight by consuming food she had deliberately hoarded and hidden earlier.
>
> It's pretty obvious that I had a problem—a serious problem. It's obvious to me today, but it wasn't then. Back then I didn't have time to recognize any problems

in my life. All I needed was another Twinkie and I could make it; I could be there for one more act of service or hour of self-sufficient sewing or canning.

The parallels between my behavior and those of an alcoholic (or a pornography addict) were terrifying and humbling. I ate in secret. I spent money that we desperately needed for family necessities on my private indulgences. The list could go on and on. I knew what it felt like to actually hate the ice cream or chocolate I was eating and still not be able to leave it alone. I knew what it meant to have every ounce of willpower I could muster fail me.

Gratefully, by the time I met and married Phil, I had been in recovery from my addiction for fifteen years and was maintaining a weight loss of over 150 pounds through the grace (power) and personal revelations of Christ (not by trying to manage or control my own behaviors). I also knew that even if Phil couldn't overcome his addiction, the Savior could, if Phil would let Him.

It helped so much for Phil and me to be able talk as two fellow mortals, equally in need of deliverance from our "thorns in the flesh." It really leveled the playing field, as the saying goes. Satan couldn't lie to me and persuade me to think that somehow I was better than Phil or that he was worse than I was. I recognized that Phil had simply fallen into a different way of trying to mood-alter than I had, when he was sad or discouraged or overwhelmed or lonely.

I know as I write this that there may be a chance that you are someone who has never struggled with a tendency to unhealthy eating, in which case you may find it as hard to relate to my story as it is for you to comprehend your husband's sexual addiction. Still, if you will honestly try, I think you will be able to identify some behavior in your life that means so much to you that you get moody and upset if you are unable to engage in it. It may be watching television, reading, spending money, or it may even be cleaning and organizing. Maybe it's exercising or trying to be perfect in some way, or maybe in every way. Remember, it could be an activity that is good when used in a healthy, moderate way, but when used to excess or in an inappropriate way, it is damaging and consuming your life.

Prayerfully consider this and ask Heavenly Father to help you discover if there are behaviors in your life that could fall under the label of addiction.

Once again, we only suggest this exercise because it is such a powerful way for a spouse to begin to comprehend in a small part that we actually share the same dilemma—we are *all* dealing with the tendencies of the **"natural man,"**[6] in one way or another. Our common enemy is Satan (not each other), and our equally in-common need is to become converted to the Lord Jesus Christ—not just to His Church—and to be **"strengthened…in the inner man"**[7] by His atoning power. Otherwise, we are all equally lost and fallen.

1. Dallin H. Oaks, "Pornography," *Ensign*, May 2005, 87.

2. Russell M. Nelson, "Addiction or Freedom," *Ensign*, Nov. 1988, 7.

3. Boyd K. Packer, "Ye Are the Temple of God," *Ensign*, Nov. 2000, 72.

4. 2 Nephi 26:22.

5. Doctrine & Covenants 123:8.

6. Mosiah 3:19.

7. Ephesians 3:16.

Chapter 3

At War Against a Common Enemy

When a home has been invaded by pornography or another sexual sin, the very foundations of a marriage can be shaken. Both partners look at the other as the source of their pain and suffering. She looks at him and says, "How could you bring such trash into our home, into our lives?" He sees her words as yet another source of shame, another reason to turn to his addiction. Love in the home is replaced by fighting and recrimination. Both people begin to wonder if their marriage will survive this dreadful division between them.

> *The battle seems futile at times. I know it is the adversary. Through this experience he has discovered my Achilles' heel and my husband's. What better way to destroy a family than to make us both wallow in the bitter battle of addiction, compulsion and obsession? I know where to turn for strength, but the futility of repeated patterns has left me tired and weak.*
> — *Lois*

Satan has established a beachhead in the family, a frontline within the home.

Colleen: Satan Wants to Destroy Both of You

One of the truths I have been most blessed by as I have allowed it to find place in my heart, is the truth that Phil and I are not each other's enemies. We are actually comrades in arms against the same enemy—Satan. Letting this truth soften my heart towards Phil was one of the most powerful contributions I made to become his ally in his recovery efforts. I can't emphasize how important it is that you begin to prayerfully consider allowing the Lord to open this witness to your heart about your husband.

In the spiritual realm, just as the Savior taught, there is a legion of evil spirits in league with Satan who desire not only your husband's destruction, but yours as well. Satan is doing all he can to turn you against each other—blaming and accusing and shaming each other. He is the one who would deluge your husband with lust and drown you in despair. He is the one who would destroy your potential as individual children of God. He is the one who would like to see you become so despondent that you develop addictions of your own as you try to cope with your fear and pain. He is the one who hopes the effects of your unhappiness will drive your children to resort to addictive behaviors.

When the addiction is revealed and recovery has a chance to begin, he often intensifies his efforts.

Maybe Satan feels we are slipping from his grasp because we are getting into recovery. He knows how to destroy our family. He can entice my husband to choose to follow him until he is an addict. He can encourage me to be so angry and resentful that I am filled with contention and have no desire to forgive. He can give me every opportunity to become thoroughly overwhelmed so that I can't mother my children—and if I can't do that, I can't protect them from his snares. — Cathy

Of all the people alive today, we as Latter-day Saints are *potentially* among the most fortunate, even when the battle with pornography has entered our homes. Why? Because of the eternal perspective on life provided to us by the doctrines of the Restoration. We say "potentially" because our doctrines do us no good if we don't learn them or, if knowing them, we don't apply them in the trenches of our real lives.

This is a spiritual war being fought in the spiritual depths of men's and women's souls. We must be willing to step back from the immediate heartache in order to see the big picture of what's really going on and to recognize our common enemy.

Drawing on Gospel Truths to Reveal Our Real Enemy

According to the scriptures, Satan was once known as Lucifer and actually began a war in heaven. This was not a war of flesh and blood, but a war of heart and mind. It was a time in which each of us decided how we felt about agency. Did we agree with Lucifer's offer to save us from the painful, messy consequences of agency? Obviously, since we're here in mortality, we agreed with Heavenly Father's plan, which required us to humble ourselves and participate in a fallen, imperfect world that we can only escape by allowing the Savior to rescue us.

When Satan's offer was not accepted, he became enraged at God and at those of us who chose to follow our Father's plan, to trust Jesus to redeem us. Satan is the one who still encourages these very same attitudes of bitterness and resentment in our hearts today. He leads us away from life on God's terms—those terms being agency, imperfection and humility. This becomes especially true when we must deal with the reality of addiction in our own life or in the lives of our loved ones.

Colleen: Coming to Know the Unfailing Love of God

The adversary is literally drowning the human family in lies. We can hardly get through an hour of our day without something discouraging and disheartening bombarding our hearts and minds with negative thoughts. Thanks to our modern media and technology, the whole world has become the equivalent of a tiny village where we can hear (almost instantly) about enough sad, traumatic things to last a lifetime! Then, to find out that the influence of the adversary has reached right into the heart of our marriages and our lives—it is enough to crush every hope we have. That is exactly what he is working for and planning on—to convince us that life isn't worth living.

When I was going through the darkest times in my first marriage, the adversary bombarded me with the lie that life wasn't worth living. The only thing that saved me was coming to the Savior, personally and directly, in the same way as did Alma the Younger.

> **I remembered also to have heard my father prophesy unto the people concerning the coming of one Jesus Christ, a Son of God, to atone for the sins of the world.**
>
> **Now, as my mind caught hold upon this thought, I cried within my heart: O Jesus, thou Son of God, have mercy on me, who am in the gall of bitterness, and am encircled about by the everlasting chains of death (Alma 36:17-18).**

Of course, in Alma's case he was suffering for his own sins, but the truth is that sin, no matter who commits it, has the potential to drag us all down into the **"gall of bitterness"** and the **"everlasting chains of death,"** unless we can turn to the Savior and call on Him for salvation.

As I went through those terrible, dark years, there was only one way and means by which I could find rest to my soul, and that was by establishing my faith securely upon the Lord Jesus Christ, Himself—not just on being a member of His true Church. Membership and activity alone were not enough to save me. I needed *Him*. I needed to come to the veil and converse with Him, sometimes every hour, in order to receive His Spirit and His guidance about what He would have me do each day.

It was also during this time that I was delivered from Satan's lie that God is a stern and punitive being who will not bless me if I am in any way unworthy or unfaithful in my own thoughts and actions. I was so grateful to learn, instead, that my Heavenly Father and my Savior are both "big" enough and spiritually secure enough to handle my anger and bitterness, even if, in the midst of my pain, I direct it toward Them. I have learned by my own experience that literally *nothing* can separate me from the love of God.[1]

Colleen: The Sacred Act of Holding Nothing Back from the Lord

Yes, you heard me correctly. It really is okay for you to admit to Heavenly Father that you're mad at Him, or at the very least, that you're really confused and frustrated toward Him and His **"great plan of happiness."**[2] After all, He knew your husband had this problem and He didn't warn you about it. It's normal to question why God didn't warn you and keep you from ending up in such a marriage.

I have learned that to harbor any negative thoughts or feelings of any kind while trying to pretend them away is to fall once again into the liar's trap. You see, the adversary doesn't want you to go to Heavenly Father with your whole heart and pour it all out—right down to the dregs, right down to the very last drop of sorrow, sadness, regret, resentment, bitterness, confusion, and anger. Satan knows that if you do, you will discover for yourself just how loving and compassionate Heavenly Father really is.

Unlike Satan, our Father will not attack you with accusations and doubts. I have every confidence that you will find, as I did, that He will continue to love you, even if you are full of anger and disgust at your husband, yourself, and even at Him, for what has happened.

Some years ago, as I was pondering what it means to fully surrender my will and my life to the Lord (as Step Three in the Twelve Step program invites us to do), I realized that I had to be willing to lay all the pain I had ever felt on the Savior's willing and capable shoulders. On that occasion, I wrote the following words in my journal:

> When I have finally come to the end of myself and I have lost the battle and given into my fear, anger, frustration, impatience and bitterness, I find nowhere to go but to the same God I'm so tempted to blame for not saving

me from "this hour." How amazed I am at the *humility* of the Lord in the face of my feelings, as I hear these words come into my mind and know they are His:

> "Let me have your pain, Colleen. Your anger and your bitterness as well."
>
> "Lay it on me. I can take it....In fact, I *have* taken it."
>
> "I'll step in between you and the pain."
>
> "I'll take a 'bullet' for you, *even if you need to fire it.* Blast away."
>
> "Get it all out. Get all the pain out."
>
> "Don't hold anything back."

The peace the Lord offers comes only when we're finally willing to *let* the Lord be the one—the only one—to save us. The greatest truth that you and your husband will ever come to know is just how much you are loved by your Savior, even in your addictions and your confusion.

Our message, as you will hear over and over in this book, is that these feelings, as well as all of your other challenges, can be taken to the Lord. His mission was and continues to be to **"bind up the broken-hearted."**[2] We hope to convey to you our sure witness that comes from personal experience: He stands ready and waiting for you to cast your burdens upon Him so that He can bear them for you.

This connection with Him is exactly what Helaman described to his sons. We offer this "likening" of Helaman's testimony. It is our testimony, as well.

> **And now, [dear sister], remember, remember *that it is upon the rock of our Redeemer, who is Christ, the Son of God, that ye must build your foundation; that when the devil shall send forth his mighty winds, yea, his shafts in the whirlwind, yea, when all his hail and his mighty***

storm shall beat upon you [in the form of all the devil's lies], **it shall have no power over you to drag you down to the gulf of misery and endless wo** (Helaman 5:12, emphasis added).

Satan is just as real as God. He wants to destroy my husband and by so doing hopes he can destroy our family unit. He is whispering things to me constantly, wanting me to feel discouraged, fearful and hopeless. I refuse to let him win! This is a burden that either I chose or the Lord chose for me to carry in this life. I don't know how it will end. I hope it will end happy and positive, but if it does not end that way, I know that before I was ever a wife to an addict, I was a daughter of God and I will always be a daughter of God! As long as I am true and faithful, He will take care of me and my family. Everything will turn out in the end. — Lynnette

---

Escaping the Lies Satan Has Snared Us With

It's interesting that Satan is called the **"father of all lies,"**[3] not the father of adultery or even the father of murder. It is also interesting that Satan thrives on secrecy—whether it be about an episode with overeating or with pornography. Once we start doing our "thing" in secret—eating, spending, or whatever—we've crossed a line into his territory and cut ourselves off from the fellowship of truth.

One of the most prevalent lies Satan perpetrates on the human family has to do with his own self—what he looks like and what he has the power to do to us. Since the beginning of all mythology and superstition, he has encouraged us to think of him in a variety of terrifying forms, holding all kinds of magical powers to cause things to happen in the physical world. In one simple statement, the Prophet Joseph Smith revealed the truth about Satan's influence:

All beings who have bodies have power over those who have not. *The devil has no power over us only as we permit him* (Cook and Ehat, *Words of Joseph Smith,* p. 60, emphasis added).

In other words, all Satan can do to harm us is whisper negative, discouraging, lie-based thoughts into our minds and hope that we will believe him and act out our beliefs toward ourselves and toward each other. That's what he did in the garden when he lied to Eve, and it is what he did when he convinced Cain to kill his brother, Abel. He lied and convinced them to take action based on those lies. And so it has been from the beginning.

[Satan] **is the father of all lies; even that same liar who beguiled our first parents, yea, even that same liar who hath caused man to commit murder from the beginning (Ether 8:25).**

If Satan can't take control of us through our fear of his power to hurt us, then he goes to the opposite extreme and tells us there is no devil: **"I am no devil, for there is none."**[4] This belief that there is no spiritual realm or spiritual influence, such as God or the devil, is the position of secular science and humanism, including social sciences, such as sociology and psychology. It is the prevailing "world view" (belief system) that we have been immersed in for the last 150 years. And we are reaping the whirlwind of the human family embracing and acting upon that lie.

And thus he whispereth in their ears, until he grasps them with his awful chains, from whence there is no deliverance [except through seeking and embracing the Atonement of Jesus Christ] **(2 Nephi 28:22).**

Satan's tactics have not changed. They can't. Even today, He can use no other tactic against us except to lie. Satan is still trying to drive the lie of blame and shame between every husband and wife like a wedge, just as he tried to do in the garden between Adam and Eve.

Colleen: Some of the Lies Satan Uses Against Women

Satan's desire is to make you miserable, to discourage and dishearten you, to bring you down in every way possible. So what are the lies he uses against you? Here is a partial list of lies I've either believed myself or heard other women express about themselves. See how many of them you recognize in your own thoughts:

- ❑ You're not pretty enough.
- ❑ You're fat.
- ❑ You're old.
- ❑ You're plain.
- ❑ You're flat.
- ❑ You're too much.
- ❑ You're not enough.
- ❑ You're the problem.
- ❑ You don't do enough.
- ❑ You don't do the right things for him in bed.
- ❑ You don't care enough.
- ❑ You don't keep yourself dolled up enough.
- ❑ You've gained weight.
- ❑ You're too skinny.
- ❑ You're the wrong size, shape, color.
- ❑ You're boring.
- ❑ You caused it, you know.
- ❑ You weren't enough to get him to stop using pornography when he married you.
- ❑ You could cure this if you'd just change.
- ❑ You can control this if you just scream at him enough.
- ❑ You can control this if you just stay up late enough and get up early enough.

❑ You can control this if you keep track of him closely enough.

❑ This wouldn't be happening if it weren't for you.

❑ He'd be a faithful husband if you just hadn't: let yourself go/gained weight/yelled at him/needed him so much.

The lies could go on and on and on and on and on. There's no end to them. As soon as you try to respond to one (by believing and obeying it), a hundred more spring up. You go on fighting, swinging, flailing, slashing, and trying to conquer the lies by fighting them. You snap at the kids. You can't open the drapes. You begin lying to everyone you meet—pretending you're fine—when inside your soul you are dying from the spiritual infection caused by these lies.

For me, it helps just to recognize where these feelings (of bitterness and discouragement) are coming from. If I can recognize that it's just the adversary working on me, it's easier to put those feelings in their place. I realize that these thoughts aren't some weak, bad part of me... This is warfare and the enemy is firing on me! If I get wounded by a bullet, I don't have to run around wondering how I could have been so silly as to get shot and blame myself for having a bullet in me. I realize that the enemy has attacked me, and I can take myself to the surgeon to be healed.   *— Margene*

Phil: Some of the Lies Satan Tells Men

Of course, women aren't the only ones Satan lies to. He lies to men just as much as to women. Some of the lies are the same—some are different. You may recognize some of these in your husband's excuses. Maybe you see them in some behavior of your own. At any rate, let's get more explicit about the lies he's telling the guys:

❑ Sex is your most important need.

- ❑ You are never going to get enough.
- ❑ No one is really going to take care of your needs.
- ❑ Even if your wife is a willing partner, you need more.
- ❑ You are being kind to her by taking care of your own needs.
- ❑ It's important that other women besides your wife find you attractive.
- ❑ You're not attractive to others.
- ❑ You're a loser.
- ❑ No girl would want you.
- ❑ Go ahead and stimulate your own sexual feelings. No one cares. No one knows. It won't matter.
- ❑ You deserve to know what it feels like.
- ❑ You deserve to know what is going on in the world.
- ❑ Go ahead and look. They're just pictures.
- ❑ You're not victimizing these women in the pictures. They enjoy expressing themselves.
- ❑ You're not hurting anyone.
- ❑ You're only hurting yourself, so it's ok.
- ❑ This is normal. All men do this.
- ❑ You're not normal if you don't look.

In *Clean Hands, Pure Heart*, I wrote about the double whammy Satan throws at men, first enticing them to sin, then shaming them for giving in.

> Satan actually twists the enticing of our own conscience to defeat us. Unlike the Lord, he doesn't respect us and he doesn't have any integrity. He doesn't fight fair. He entices us to sin, saying, "Hey, this will be fun, this will be great–come and try this out! It's not that bad. It won't do any harm." Then when we give in, he turns on us and

sneers in our face, in a cruel, sadistic imitation of our
conscience: "You sinner! You scum! You are the biggest
slime ball in history. No one could possibly tolerate you
(let alone love you) if they knew what you are *really*
like." On and on it goes. Is it any wonder the adversary
is referred to as **"the accuser of our brethren"
(Revelation 12:10)**? The really sad part is that after a
while, we take up the cry ourselves, becoming our own
accusers. Our enemy has convinced us to join his side
against ourselves, exactly as he intended. He knows if he
can confuse our perception of our conscience enough, if
he can get us to *identify ourselves* as sinners, we are that
much easier to coax into sin. We act as we believe, and
if we believe ourselves to be bad, we are much more
likely to act badly. We say to ourselves: "Why shouldn't I
do (whatever)? That's just the sort of person I am.
There's no point in expecting anything better from me."
Thus our negative beliefs contribute to our own defeat.
As the scriptures tell us, **"For as he thinketh in his
heart, so is he" (Proverbs 23:7).**

Too often, when we are in a marriage, we look to the other person
for our strength and inspiration and are disappointed when we find that
they are just as human as we are. This can lead us to look elsewhere to
things that can become addictions for both the husband and the wife. It
doesn't matter to the adversary which direction he takes to bring us into
bondage, as long as he gets us away from the truth.

Phil: Satan's Lie That You Are Each Other's Ultimate Source

As I've counseled with my brethren over the years, I've observed
that some men—I believe under the influence of Satan—begin to twist
the often rehearsed idea that women are spiritually superior to men into
an excuse to indulge in their baser inclinations. This tendency to put
women on a pedestal is further reinforced by the cultural stereotype that
women are, by nature, more spiritually sensitive or spiritually inclined

than men. This generalization has been portrayed for years in the media, as movies and television series have shown the wife taking the children to church while the husband stays home. We often repeat statements like, "Behind every good man is a *really* good woman," or "My wife is my better half," thus implying that the wife is expected to carry the spiritual load. Even in the Church this attitude is encouraged, despite the fact that it is the husband who represents the Lord and His priesthood in the family.

I have to seriously wonder how this stereotype contributes to the way a married man addicted to pornography may shift the responsibility for his addiction to his wife, expecting her to keep him on the spiritual strait and narrow. On the other hand, I also have to wonder how much the stereotype contributes to the way a woman often believes that it is her mission to rescue her husband from himself and feels like it's her failure if he doesn't reform.

As always, the best antidote for a lie is the truth. The truth about a man and woman who share the sacred covenant of marriage is that neither of them qualifies to be the source of inspiration and power to the other. The truth is neither of you belongs on any pedestal. You are equally mortal, equally lost and equally fallen "fellows" in this life. Thus you are both *equally* in need of a spiritual rebirth into a close, personal relationship with the Savior.

The major healing that needs to happen in your life and in your husband's life will only begin when you both stop looking to each other for salvation and look to Jesus Christ instead. Only in Him will either of you find the strength and wisdom (personal revelation) to protect you against the adversary, the father of all lies.

Colleen: We Are Not the "Power Behind the Throne"

I can hardly contain the desire to testify to you, dear sister, of how important it is for us wives to realize that our husbands have a Savior *and it isn't us!*

Assuming that somehow I was in charge of saving my husband, I remained in my first marriage for years after I realized how far into sin my husband's addiction had taken him. I look back at my journal entries written during those years, and my heart breaks for the woman who wrote them. I was convinced I couldn't leave. Why? Because it was my fault he was this messed up. Why? Because I believed that what you might call "mother-power" or "woman-power" was the *ultimate* power in the family.

In other words, I believed that *I* set the mood in my home, and if the mood wasn't positive, somehow I had failed. This thinking locked me into living with a man who behaved like a peevish, mean-spirited, cruel child in the privacy of our home—toward myself and our children. All the while, I thought his moods were my fault, because I wasn't good enough to fulfill and inspire him. I truly believed the rhetoric I heard about how the woman is "the real power behind the throne," and that every worthy, well-functioning man in the Church owed to his wife his ability to perform his duties. The fact that my husband was never called to be in a bishopric, for example, was my failure.

How grateful I am to Phil for *not* putting me on a pedestal, and for *not* making me the one to whom he attributes his faithfulness, either in the fulfillment of his priesthood responsibilities or in the ongoing miracle of his abstinence from pornography addiction. It feels like the most compassionate and loving attitude I have ever felt from any man. It gives me the freedom to work out the only salvation I have the response-ability to work out—my own.

1. Romans 8:38-39.

2. Isaiah 61:1.

3. 2 Nephi 2:18.

4. 2 Nephi 28:22.

Chapter 4

I Didn't Ask for This!

Hi, Phil here. I'd like to open this discussion by sharing a memory of an incident that happened a few years ago while I was passing through the airport on my way to a short business trip.

With only two days to go until Thanksgiving, it wasn't surprising that I found the parking lot of the Salt Lake City International Airport filled to capacity, forcing me to park in the section furthest from the terminal. The shuttle was just as crowded, but the young couple in the seat across from me seemed oblivious. He wore his dark hair in a short, well-groomed haircut; her blond hair was pulled back in a neat pony tail. He was handsome; she was radiant. Over and over, her adoring, trusting gaze returned to his face. Her left hand bore a single ring with a diamond. Each of them had only a small carry-on bag with them.

Their story seemed apparent. They were headed home, either to his parents or hers. Perhaps this was the very first visit home they had made together. There would surely be excited and hopeful introductions—the beginning of a new life, a new family, with new relationships all around.

After passing through the security gates, I saw them again, sitting at a table in the food court. She was still looking at him as if there wasn't another person on the planet. The hope and adoration in her eyes could no more be hid than the rays of the sun on a clear summer morning. It was so obvious that she was willing, even eager, to entrust the rest of her life to him, along with her hopes for an eternal marriage. Into his hands she was placing all her dreams—for herself, for the two of them, and for their children to come.

Painfully aware as I am of the growing plague of pornography addiction among men—even the nicest of young men—I couldn't help wondering how this young couple's future would unfold. I struggled with questions she most likely hadn't even considered. Would her dreams be safe with him? Would he be the strong, reliable husband and lover she envisioned? Or would their happiness be challenged and perhaps shattered by the future revelation of this hidden weakness? Perhaps it was already part of his life but a part as yet undisclosed. Or it might not develop until later, after a few months or years of marriage.

If this heartbreaking situation happened to her, how would she cope with it? How could she ever see it as anything except a horrible tragedy? And if she were to be confronted with such a challenging reality, would their marriage weather the blow? Would he have the humility to admit his frailty, and furthermore, his need for help beyond his own resources? And if he did, what would be her response? Would she be willing to suffer through a painful and uncertain period of repentance and recovery? On the other hand, what if he refused to acknowledge the seriousness of his behavior? What would she do then?

Colleen: Experiencing Your Own Version of 9/11

If you were anywhere near a television on September 11, 2001, like me, you saw the video replay over and over again of the World Trade Center twin towers in New York City collapsing into a heap of rubble— 110 stories disintegrating in just over 10 seconds. I cannot think of any better comparison to what it feels like when an active LDS woman finds out that her husband is deliberately seeking and using pornography.

Learning that your husband has a sexual addiction can feel a lot like facing your own personal 9/11. Your trust and security has been destroyed and your life will never be the same again. In just a few moments, your hope and faith in him, in yourself, and in your marriage have crumbled to dust, just like the twin towers. You can't quit playing the "tape" over and over in your mind: Your husband is sexually active, sexually involved—without you.

Maybe you had no idea. You assumed that his fidelity to your marriage was as unwavering as your own. Or maybe you already had some clue that sometime in the past he'd indulged just a little, "experimented" with some form of sexual transgression. If it was in his youth, you were sure that, just as he had sworn to you, the transgression was ancient history, a problem conquered and left behind long ago. You both wanted to believe that it was something he would never think of doing again now that he had you—the girl, the wife of his dreams.

But then the day came when either a long trail of little uneasy moments or a single major discovery revealed to you that the problem is not ancient history. It is here. It is now. The truth hits you like the airplanes hit the twin towers: He is caught in the secret soul-sickness of pornography and masturbation. You confront him. You sob. You rage. You become insane trying to police his life. Over and over again, he either pledges reform with tears and sorrow or responds with defensiveness and criticism of you. Each of you begins to find bitterness replacing the love you once felt.

Or maybe, by the time you find out about his addiction, it has already escalated, seared his conscience, and enslaved his heart and mind to the point that he has actually acted out with another person. He's had an affair or paid a prostitute—all while you were being faithful, believing, and trusting.

Suddenly, all your trust turns to humiliation and the mutilation of your heart. Your own sanity feels like it's hanging by a thread. You walk numbly through your days, dealing with the children, going about your routine like a zombie. Nothing seems real or tangible any longer. It feels like your life is over, like something in you has died, and rightfully so.

In the Book of Mormon, Jacob, the brother of Nephi and a great prophet in his own right, declares how severely a husband's sexual infidelity—even if only in thought and intent—can affect his wife.

Speaking to men who were just "beginning to labor in sin," or in other words, just beginning to contemplate acting out, Jacob said:

> **Ye have broken the hearts of your tender wives, and lost the confidence of your children, because of your bad examples before them; and the sobbings of their hearts ascend up to God against you. And because of the strictness of the word of God, which cometh down against you,** *many hearts died, pierced with deep wounds* **(Jacob 2:35, emphasis added).**

Two Ways That Many Wives React to Such Deep Wounds

We've heard from many sisters who write to express one or the other of a pretty polarized reaction to finding out their husband is infected with pornography addiction. Some react by drawing away in disgust and adamantly insisting, "This is totally *his* problem. I don't want to hear about it. I don't even want to know it exists. I just want him to stay away from me until he is 100% fixed. Then, we'll see whether we have a marriage left or not."

Meanwhile, other wives become obsessed with helping their husbands stay abstinent. This wife may think in terms of a team effort: "This is *our* problem, and *we* need to do something about it." In reality, she has decided she needs to be his coach, manager, and the cheerleader of the team. Such wives remind their husbands of meetings and insist on reading recovery literature *to* them. Their belief is, "I've got to make sure he does whatever it takes. He'll never make it without me." If this is the way you feel and believe, we have some tough news for you. If your husband can't make it without you, he definitely won't make it with you, or even *for* you. His motivation has got to go deeper than keeping you pleased with him or keeping you off his back. Until you step out of the way and get on with your own spiritual growth, he won't even get started at owning his own problem or his own recovery.

No matter what your feelings about being involved in your husband's problem, we feel it is important to recognize and validate the feelings you're dealing with. This challenge can't help but affect your own sense of stability and even your feelings of sanity, as you find yourself spinning into what is often called the "cycle of addiction."

Caught in the Cycle of Addiction

Living with an addict can be a disheartening, bewildering, and agonizing experience. Sometimes he may be grouchy, angry, and just plain impossible to live with. At other times he may be very sweet and attentive. You may find yourself asking, "Which of these men is really my husband? To whom am I really married?"

It may help to know that addiction typically follows a pretty predictable pattern that goes something like this:

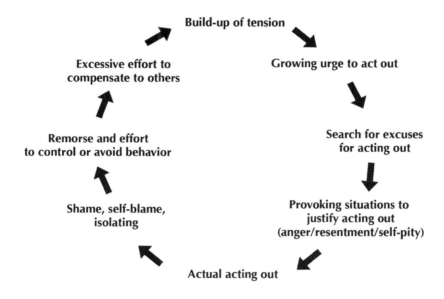

When you see this cycle of addiction continually repeating itself, you may be tempted to ask, "Is my husband really trying to overcome this addiction, or is he just trying to get around me so he can keep acting out?" Or you're tempted to think, "He doesn't *really* want to quit. If he did, things would change. I would at least be able to see some improvement." This can be a seriously inaccurate assumption.

Colleen: Your Husband's Remorse May Really Be Sincere

The concept of addiction may still be so new to you that you're having a very, very hard time believing it is the equivalent of an infection—an illness that your husband has contracted, rather than something that is plaguing him. In reality, your husband may be desperately sincere when he goes through the remorseful phase of the cycle and may be trying to stop with all the willpower he can muster—which is obviously totally inadequate.

During the phase in which he is making excessive efforts to compensate, it is most likely that he is trying to genuinely make up for how much he hurts you when the insanity of his addiction sets in. The truth is, he isn't creating this cycle of addiction; he's just as caught in this Dr. Jekyll/Mr. Hyde curse as you are. Somewhere deep inside, at a spiritual level, he is very likely feeling just as terrified of its power to destroy your life together as you are. Trying to understand this truth does not excuse him for what he's doing nor does it make it okay for him to ignore it and pretend it's not happening, but it does offer you some release from feeling that you're causing it or that you can do something to stop it.

Men who are trying to come back to peace with God, to heal and live in a marriage as God intended, may have moments when they slip. But, if they do, they will get right back "on the wagon." If you see your husband doing this, hang on to him. He's a man worth walking through hellfire with. Why? Because he is working toward wellness.   — *Tabitha*

Nevertheless, because of the heart-deep connection that marriage represents, you cannot help but be pulled into the vortex of this insane way of life and become obsessed yourself. Satan is trying to infect you with depression and despair. One of Satan's most powerful ways of doing this is getting you to believe one or both of the following ideas: 1) that you did something to deserve such a challenge, and/or 2) that you made a mistake when you married your husband.

What Did I Do to Deserve This?

A little reflection will reveal that this kind of self-incrimination is based on the false assumption that life's challenges are God's punishments. This is a lie. Satan wants you to believe Heavenly Father is deliberately meting out the heartache and pain you are feeling. It just simply is not true. The scriptures are full of examples of individuals being faced with unjust and unfair situations they did not bring on themselves or deserve.

Still, we understand that it is virtually impossible at first—and maybe for weeks and months to come—to keep the thought from going through your mind: "What did I do to deserve this? This reprehensible turn of events certainly wasn't what I signed up for. I was certain we'd have a home filled with security and love, not this sordid, evil presence in our lives that seems to be destroying us from the inside out. This isn't what my life was supposed to be like! It's so *unjust!*"

The question of what is fair or of having to face and endure your husband's addiction may be particularly powerful in your mind, especially if you've made considerable effort to live your life the best you know how—with daily personal and family prayer, scripture study, family home evenings, and church and temple attendance (or at least the goal of a temple marriage). After all, that was supposed to be *the* formula that would provide immunity against a life filled with such heartache as you now feel.

On the other hand, maybe your own choices haven't always been ideal. Maybe you have made some mistakes along the way—even serious mistakes. Perhaps mistreatment or abuse in your childhood or in past relationships has taught you to think so poorly of yourself that you have concluded that marriage to a sex addict is a just result and it is all that you deserve, the most you can hope for.

Whether you think you deserve what's happening or not, we want to adamantly bear our testimony to you: *your husband's addiction has absolutely nothing to do with your past or current behaviors or choices.*

This is not about what you do or don't deserve! This is about living in the last days and facing the challenges those days bring. The temptations and climate of today's world are filled with sexual images. That is a definite challenge to most men and also to many women. Those who succumb to these temptations are not bad people. They are mortal and have succumbed to the drives of the mortal body. Understanding this reality doesn't mean we simply accept such transgression as normal; but on the other hand, we need not overreact either.

Colleen: I Thought I Was Inspired to Marry Him

It is my testimony to you that finding yourself in the challenging situation of being married to a man addicted to pornography does not mean you weren't led by the hand of the Lord to marry him. The scriptures are full of examples of people who followed the Lord and still found themselves in the midst of great challenges. One of the greatest symbolic examples of this can be found in Lehi's dream:

> **And it came to pass that I saw a man, and he was dressed in a white robe; and he came and stood before me. And it came to pass that he spake unto me, and bade me follow him. And it came to pass that as I followed him *I beheld myself that I was in a dark and dreary waste* (1 Nephi 8:5-7, emphasis added).**

Here we find that Lehi followed an angel representing the Lord and, of all things, he found himself in a "dark and dreary waste." What? How could that be? And yet it is right there in black and white.

I can't tell you how many times between seminary, institute classes, and family scripture reading, I had read those verses and totally missed that amazing insight. Following the Lord doesn't guarantee a fairy tale outcome. Yet, I had bought into that fallacy completely and I had married fully expecting that my activity in the Church would insure safety from "the dark and dreary" influences of the world.

It was only when I turned back to the Book of Mormon, desperately needing to hear and see the truths it contained that would get me closer to God than any other book or source of advice I could find, that I began to have eyes to see and a heart to understand such mysteries. Only then did I absorb the example of Lehi's faithfulness to the Lord, despite the fact that He didn't just whisk Lehi and his family away to the **"far better land of promise."**[1]

No, Lehi walked thousands of miles and put up with years and years of challenges. He definitely went through a "dark and dreary waste" experience before he arrived in the place the Lord first revealed to him as his "promised land." It was then that I realized that the Lord reserves the right to require the same of me. I faced a huge call to step up to the plate when I saw that obedience to the Lord doesn't bring the same type of instant results as putting a dollar in a vending machine.

I believe that, without exception, we will all face at least one trial in this life that is going to exceed our capacity to deal with it. In other words, we are all going to face our own version of a Gethsemane experience. We're all going to have to come to a place where we find ourselves pleading with the Father, even as our Savior did, "Let this cup pass from me. Please don't let this thing be happening. Please, God, don't let it be true. I can't face this. I can't deal with it. Please take it away. *Please* turn the clock back. What did I do to end up like this?"

Seeking the Savior's Ability to Separate the Sin from the Sinner

We often hear the scripture rehearsed that states, **"For I the Lord cannot look upon sin with the least degree of allowance,"**[2] to imply that if a person is committing any kind of sin, God cannot stand to look upon him or her, and the person must stop sinning before He will embrace them. This is such a sad interpretation of that verse, and with just a little thought, I believe, we can see its fallacy. In His earthly ministry, Jesus "looked upon" sinners continuously. He walked with them, talked with them, touched them—lepers, cripples, harlots, wine bibbers, money-changers, to name just a few of the sinners He invited into His life. All of us are sinners; there are no perfect people for Jesus to look upon.

> **Wherefore, all mankind were in a lost and in a fallen state, and ever would be save they should rely on this Redeemer (1 Nephi 10:6).**

None of us can escape needing the Savior's merciful willingness to receive us just as we are—infected with one kind of sin or another. While there is no doubt that pornography is a great evil, we must remember that nowhere is there a greater need for us to distinguish between condemning the sin and annihilating the sinner.

In counseling the Saints about the war Satan would rage against us in these last days, the Prophet Joseph Smith advised us to exercise caution in attacking evil too hastily:

> **Stay yourselves; do not give way** [to Satan's urging to attack those who have done wrong]; **don't make any hasty moves, you may be saved.** *If a spirit of bitterness is in you, don't be in haste.* **You may say, that man is a sinner. Well, if he repents, he shall be forgiven. Be cautious, await** (Joseph Smith, *History of the Church,* 6:314-15, emphasis added).

It may help you feel the truth of the Prophet Joseph's counsel if you take a few minutes to remember the feelings you had toward your husband in the early days of your courtship and marriage. Why did you marry this man? Wasn't there a lot of good in him that made you want to give yourself to him in marriage? And now, because you have found a flaw, are you tempted to throw the whole deal overboard? That's like saying because there's a hole in the dike, the dike is useless—so condemn it. Or because there's a leak in the boat, take a hatchet to it.

Here is a verse that plainly demonstrates that it is possible for a man to administer in a righteous manner for the sake of others who depend on him, but to still be cut off from the Lord in his own spiritual life:

> **And he did do justice unto the people, but not unto himself because of his many whoredoms; wherefore he was cut off from the presence of the Lord (Ether 10:11).**

The truth is, for the most part, our brethren—including our husbands—who have been sent into the world in these last days, are good men facing a challenging problem. Good men. Sons of God. Saved for the last days, when the battles would be the fiercest.

Colleen: Getting Past the Feelings of Devastation

Now, with all that said, let's get back to the other side of the paradoxical reality you live with. While this challenge of your husband's addiction is not your fault, it would be untrue, unfair, and unfeeling to suggest that it doesn't affect you.

> *My biggest problem is that I am afraid that as soon as something good starts to happen he will quit doing everything (praying, reading, seeing his counselor, etc.) and then the cycle will begin again.* — Judy

It's only natural and understandable that you have spent hours obsessed with doubt and confusion over this issue. You have every right to these feelings. To get out of them, to move past them, however, you must eventually stop indulging them and ask yourself what you are going to do with them. To act upon them by attacking something, whether it's your husband or your "to do" list or the extra pounds you need to lose, is not the same as finding release and genuine peace.

I would like to propose that it is likely that even before you were born, you had an idea of what you were getting into when you entered mortality. You knew earth life would be hard and that even your closest loved ones would be capable of making choices that would hurt you. In other words, you knew you were headed for a **"dark and dreary waste"**[3] when you chose the Father's plan and followed the Savior into this mortal experience.

Pray about this—about whether you knew and trusted Heavenly Father and Jesus before you were born. Pray about whether you were shown that mortality in these last days might very likely include this kind of challenge and whether or not you were willing to face it.

I feel assured that you will receive the witness that you and your husband were both willing to accept this degree of challenge that is so prevalent in these last days. I also know, because I have lived it myself, that this witness will bring with it an increase of compassion for both yourself and your husband, as one. The Lord loves you both and desires to save you and your marriage if at all possible.

I have learned that I may be pushed to my very limits, to where I think I can't go another minute. Much learning, growth and strength come from those moments. I also know that when I truly am to my limit, the Lord provides a way for me to be lifted to where I am okay again. I know that I agreed to this life before I came here. ... I know that no matter what I do or what opportunities the Lord gives my husband, it is ultimately his responsibility to choose righteousness. — Terri

---

1. Alma 37:45.

2. Doctrine & Covenants 1:31.

3. 1 Nephi 8:7.

Chapter 5

If Only
I Were Better

When a wife finds out for certain that her husband is viewing pornography, the injury she experiences takes on even deeper dimensions than when she just suspected. While that terrible stage of wondering, "Is he or isn't he?" is finally over, now there is the feeling of being devalued and betrayed, even if the "other women" have only been flat, two dimensional images on a computer screen, video, or magazine.

Once Satan has made that inroad into a woman's sense of self-worth, he immediately begins to bombard her with shame and guilt. "It's your fault," he lies. "It's because you're not enough for him. It's because you're too skinny...or too fat. It's because you're not giving him enough attention. It's because you're not doing enough to make your home a pleasant place..." On and on go the lies—and we as wives fall into a terrible, heartbreaking despair because of them.

In this chapter we will confront some of those lies. We pray that our testimony of the truth will find a place in and be a balm to your heart.

Colleen: The Impulse to Blame Yourself

Unfortunately, one of the first reactions a woman has when she learns of her husband's pornography problem, or learns that it is still a problem, is to assume there must be something lacking in her, or something that she's doing or not doing that is causing him to need to indulge in such behavior. As if these personal thoughts weren't devastating enough, often others (family members or priesthood leaders) will hint at it or even outright suggest this to be the case.

This train of thought is a total fallacy. If pursued and believed, it leads to even more heartache. You must be grounded in the truth to avoid this lie, to ignore it when it comes to your mind, and to forgive others who thoughtlessly suggest it to you.

> I believed that if my spouse wanted to be with me, I must be okay or desirable or valued. If he didn't, I wasn't worthy, etc. Gradually, I began to realize that my looking to man for my worth had replaced my looking to God. For if I had looked to Him as I ought, I would have been unwavering and [seen] the truth about my worth.   —Tina

In the late 1980s, I went to my bishop for the very first time concerning my first husband's sexual addiction and indiscretions. The bishop listened attentively enough, but I know he was totally broadsided by my disclosure. How could this be possible? How could this man who never missed a Sunday meeting, who was serving in responsible priesthood positions, be doing something like this? Surely, something must be lacking in his marriage, in his intimate relationship with his wife. That was the bishop's first effort to make sense of what he was hearing. Point blank, he asked me, "Colleen, are you sure you're taking care of his...his 'needs'?"

To have the responsibility for your husband's choice laid on your shoulders is a tragedy. But it's easy to see why this thought is common among us. The popular press and media are constantly promoting the idea that if a woman doesn't keep herself attractive and available to her husband, she can't really blame him for having a wandering eye and mind. The exhausted, preoccupied wife and mother have always been a stereotype and the butt of a great deal of derisive humor. If she can't compete with whatever the current version of "ideal" happens to be, she can just about count on losing her husband—and of course it's all her fault. This is an unjust and outright evil attitude that our culture cultivates toward women. It's time we start undoing these unfair, one-sided concepts of man-woman, husband-wife relations. There is absolutely no place for them in the light of the Restored Gospel.

In stark contrast, the truth found in the scriptures and teachings of the prophets gives a very different perspective on just what the marriage covenant expects of a husband. The Lord says, **"Thou shalt love thy wife with all thy heart, and shalt cleave unto her and *none else.*"**[1]

Despite what modern society portrays, the Lord didn't put an escape clause in that phrase. He didn't add "unless she puts on too much weight," or "unless she is tired at the end of the day (from taking care of your children, by the way)," or "unless you find someone who is more attractive." In the eyes of the Lord, total fidelity after marriage is the standard. If your husband chooses not to fulfill his covenant, it is not your responsibility. There is nothing—*absolutely nothing*—that the Lord takes as an excuse from your husband for his unfaithfulness toward you. His decision to be unfaithful to you is due to a lack in him, not in you.

Phil: A Man's Faithfulness Has *Nothing* to Do With His wife

If you are still tempted to believe the lie that if you were just more glamorous or voluptuous or thinner or younger, you could ensure his faithfulness, I'd like to propose that you consider for a moment the plight of the vast majority of famous female entertainers and supermodels. If physical attractiveness were what kept a man faithful to his wife, you would think these women, acclaimed as the most beautiful women in our society, would have the most secure, long-lasting marriages. Is that what we see? Far from it. Reports of infidelity blaze across the front pages of the tabloids on display in every grocery store.

Similar stories are the fare of gossip columns in newspapers, magazines, and entertainment news programs on radio and television. Let us say it again: *Fidelity in a man is not a reflection of his wife. It is a reflection of himself and his own character.*

Now let's take a minute to contrast this example with another group of men and women—the General Authorities of the Church and their wives. Here we find women who represent the life-style you have chosen—that of homemaker, wife and mother. We love them, admire them, and watch them as, along with their husbands, they epitomize the best of the Gospel and Christ-centered living. We consider them beautiful, whether they be old or young, tall or short, thin or "fluffy."

However, even more important to take note of, sisters, is how their husbands regard them—with absolute loyalty and adoration. Once again, may I repeat the truth, hoping and praying that you will allow some of it to penetrate to your heart: The choice these men make to be faithful and loyal to their wives and to keep their eyes and minds in check is about their own integrity. It is a choice *they* have made. It is a choice they remake, either consciously or unconsciously, every time they are in the presence of another woman. In the heart and mind of such a man, there is only one woman—the one who has given herself to him to be his eternal companion, his wife and only lover. This principle and standard is given powerful scriptural expression:

> **Wherefore, my brethren, hear me, and hearken to the word of the Lord: For there shall not any man among you have save it be one wife; and concubines he shall have none (Jacob 2:27).**

Phil: Even an Affair Is a Lie and Nothing to Envy

I am grateful to say that I cannot speak from personal experience about having an affair, but I have worked as a Twelve Step recovery sponsor with men who have committed adultery. In every case, I have seen this truth: an affair is nothing more than a *three-dimensional* illusion.

If your husband has allowed his addiction to take him into a physical affair, please don't let Satan fool you into believing that he is actually having a two-way, in-depth relationship. His affair is no more real than the guys who are "only" doing pornography and masturbation. An affair is still nothing but a flight into a fantasy world where he gets to exercise his lust. Both parties are using each other to escape the challenges and responsibility that come along with participating in a genuine, real-life relationship. Having an affair is no more the equivalent of being married than is playing house. Illicit, on-the-sly sex is nothing like love-making in a celestial marriage.

Comparing Yourself: Another Tragic Impulse

> *When I compare myself I get in trouble. I am trying to learn to love myself and see the beauty that Heavenly Father sees. He doesn't make ugly things. This is really hard. As hard as forgiveness. But I'll keep trying.*   — Irene

Many, if not most, wives have had very little exposure to pornography previous to finding their husbands' cache of website links or stored pictures, whether online, in printed form or on DVDs. When a woman does get her first look at what he's been viewing, we are back to the shock of watching the twin towers collapse.

> *Just knowing the thoughts he has is bad enough but then to also have the images and the memories playing over and over again—it is a catastrophic mind-numbing heart-wrenching experience.*   — Margene

You are repulsed and riveted at the same time. Sometimes you flip the off switch immediately, but often, for many of us, there's the temptation to go back and see more. The tragic result of this impulse is that you can't get those images out of your mind. Why? Because they have infected you with a kind of obsession or lust, too. You can't stop comparing yourself to those images. You can't look in a mirror. You can't get undressed. You can't endure being aware of your own body because it isn't like the images you can't forget. In other words, you can't appreciate or respect your own body because it doesn't look like those images. Satan has now set up a powerful battlefront in *your* mind and heart, as well as in your husband's.

> *When I first found out about my husband's addiction, I felt so awful about myself. I became very critical. I would not let him see me naked. The lights were always out in the bedroom at night. I didn't even want him to see me in my pajamas.*
> — *Cheryl*

Here again, your only defense against Satan's attack is to arm yourself with the truth and pray for the Spirit of Truth to recall it to your mind as many times a day as you may need to remember it: *those images are not real women.*

Even if those images began with photographs of real women, they have been altered—first with make-up and then with air-brushing and other photographic adjustments and digital enhancements. The true body of the original model does not look like those images either.

Colleen: Believing the Witness of the Truth

Many wives worry that when they are being intimate with their husbands, their husbands are fantasizing about the women they've seen while viewing pornography. They wonder if having sexual relations with their husband is just providing him with another form of acting out. When Phil and I began to calmly discuss his pornography addiction, he was adamant in affirming to me the witness I had already felt from the Lord, that this "disease" in his life had nothing to do with me personally.

Phil explained to me that though it might be hard for me to understand, his involvement with pornography was not even an involvement with people real to him. They were just what they looked like—flat, two-dimensional images that caused a certain reaction in his body, a reaction that he had become addicted to as a teenager. In other words, like so many men addicted to pornography, his craving for it was not a reaction to any deficit in Kathy, his first wife, or in me. *The deficit he was trying to fill existed in his heart and mind long before he met either of us.*

Phil: Your Husband Can Come to Know the Lord's Love for You

I'd like to add my witness to Colleen's testimony of this truth. The adversary is trying to destroy you when he entices you to compare yourself to the images perpetrated on all of us through the porn industry. These images don't depict real people. They are images of dreams, of illusions, and they represent your husband's addiction *not* to another woman, but to the chemical, physiological reaction of his body.

I can testify to you that the images are hardly even perceived as human. They are just a means to an end, as the saying goes—and the end or result the man craves is the chemical, hormonal, mood-altering effect of the images. It's just like heroin, taken in through the eyes instead of through the veins.

It's not uncommon for a pornography addict to click from one image to another, spending only seconds on each one. Believe me, what your husband feels for those images is lust, *not* love. What he's experiencing, as the stranglehold of addiction deepens in his life, is not even in the same realm as what you and he have shared. It is slavery and bondage, and it eventually becomes a form of hellish torture.

Some women think the way to help their husband is to compete with what he is seeing in the pornographic images. That is exactly what Satan wants you to do. He's the one whispering into your mind that you need to look more like the pornographic images.

Do not go into the enemy's territory to try to win your husband back. To care for yourself enough to keep up with your own hygiene and health in a reasonable manner is one thing, but to try to make a drastic change in your appearance through extreme measures is like saying, "The porn industry's right. That's how women should look and that's how they should think and act."

That is the world's view—that a woman must fit some arbitrary standard of beauty or appearance. Don't fall for it. Be yourself. You are enough as you are.

As a man gets further into recovery and takes on more and more of the Savior's personality and perspective, he will come to see you and know you as the Lord sees you and knows you.

As I continued believing in and practicing the principles of recovery, I found myself filled with the Lord's love for Colleen and His esteem for her. It had absolutely nothing to do with her looks. I am often brought to tears with tenderness and appreciation for her. The miracle is that the feeling is mutual. She tells me often that she knows the love she feels for me—which is so kind and patient with my frailties—is actually a portion of the Lord's own love for me.

We both recognize that we are living a miracle in the charity we feel for each other. We know that it is Christ's own love for each of us passing between us. This is the love a true marriage is founded on. We know that you and your husband can survive this crisis you're facing, too, and actually be *more* in love than ever before, if you will both seek to have a relationship with the Lord first and each other second.

1. Doctrine & Covenants 42:22; emphasis added.

6

I Need to Watch Him Constantly

I'm always watching his every move. When we're out in public, when we watch TV, when we read the newspaper, after he's been on the internet, etc, etc. I can't seem to stop doing that. I know it isn't fair to either one of us for me to be tracking his every movement. — Tina

As a woman who has lived through the experience of losing myself (and almost my sanity) trying to be my first husband's conscience, I'd like to invite you to take another look at the chart we included in our first discussion about what it means to be addicted (p. 15).

The terrifying thing is that the spouse (or other loved one) of an addict can be plunged right into the fourth or fifth stages of this progressive illness. In other words we, as wives, can become compulsive and obsessive in relationship to our husband's addiction immediately upon learning about it. The addiction isn't ours, but for all living purposes it becomes ours through our inability to discern where our agency leaves off and his begins.

Think about how ironic and almost insane it really is that while your husband feels compelled to keep watching porn, you feel compelled to keep watching him. While he can't stop lusting after it or feeling destroyed and enslaved by it, you can't stop thinking about what he's doing, or what he has done, or what he might yet do. When you're not thinking about him, you're thinking about yourself and how you compare to the women in the porn. On and on and on it goes, around and around, spinning out of control, spiraling ever further into desperation, until you can hardly participate in a normal life.

How hard is it to put down your obsession about what he's doing? Do you find it virtually impossible? Does it feel like it has taken on a life of its own? Does it follow you and torment you and torture you to the point that you can't stop thinking about it? To the point that the rest of your life is overshadowed and even damaged by it? Welcome to the Satan's snare. What started out as you trying to act as your husband's conscience has trapped you in what has been called "co-addiction," or "codependency." He lusts after porn. You lust after his recovery. And Satan rejoices in both his bondage *and* yours.

Years ago, while reading *A Codependent's Guide to the Twelve Steps* by Melodie Beattie, I came across her astounding story of the lengths she went to, trying to get her drug-addicted boyfriend to realize how much he was hurting her. Though she had been clean and sober from drugs and alcohol for quite a while herself, she found herself still suffering from his choice to keep using. She set up a situation where she pretended she had started using again and had overdosed. When he nearly went into hysterics, trying to revive her, she jumped up off the couch, rejoicing in his pain and demanding that he acknowledge that he was scaring her and hurting her that way *every* day.

Recently, I read the account of an LDS woman who, upon finding an X-rated video her husband had brought home, proceeded to go down to the video store herself and rent a bunch more just like it, so she could have them stacked on the kitchen table when he came home. That was her way of confronting and shaming him.

To me, both of these stories illustrate people behaving in irrational ways to try to stop irrational behavior in their loved ones. There is one very important difference, though. In Melodie Beattie's story, she is confessing the insanity of her attempt to control the irrational actions of her loved one by resorting to an irrational act herself. In the case of the second story, the woman who went to the video store and rented a bunch of X-rated videos is heralded as having done something inspired and noble, going to any length to get through to her husband, to show him just how shameful his actions had become.

My heart aches for this sister who was so desperate to stop her husband that she thought shaming him like that would bring him to his senses. If there is any truth that I have learned from living my own life and trying to raise children, it is that shaming someone will backfire every time.

I hope you'll believe me when I say this: You don't have to get your husband's attention about how disgusting and shameful his choices are. He knows that already, and paradoxically, knowing it has the opposite effect you want to see in him. Shame doesn't give him courage to give it up, it drags him further into it.

Addiction does have a life of its own—and that life is Satan's presence. He revels in encouraging every bit of degradation he can whisper into his victim's mind. Remember he is the one who wants your husband to think, "You're scum, all right. You might as well go ahead and do what scum does."

Colleen: Putting Pressure on Him Will Backfire

As backwards as it may sound, the less you try to do to get him to change, the greater the chance that he *will* change. Why? Because the more responsibility you try to assume for his behavior, the less responsibility he will feel for himself. He may even rationalize his acting out by saying, "Well, she didn't stop me…" Or he may become resentful and act out just to prove that he still has his agency.

We fought a war to defend that principle, remember? It runs pretty deep within us. The feeling that we don't want to be controlled is very strong. Trying to control someone's behavior is not the best way to help them. Look at how Heavenly Father "raises" us. He teaches us principles through the prophets, then remains in the background and lets us decide when we are willing to live them.

It may help to remember what experts advise us to do if we wake up while on a camping trip in the mountains with a grizzly bear breathing in our face. Remain very still! Even though it may seem an illogical and terrifying thing to do, this is a time when being "still" is vital. A most powerful version of this counsel came to me when the Lord helped me to apply a scripture to my own panic about my husband's addiction:

> **Therefore, dearly beloved brethren, let us** *cheerfully* [or at least *calmly*] **do all things that lie in our power; and then** [when we have come to the end of our capacity to remain calm] **may we stand still, with the utmost assurance, to see the salvation of God, and for his arm to be revealed (Doctrine & Covenants 123:17, emphasis added).**

Now, this is not to say that we shouldn't be calmly going about doing all we can to prevent evil, but the operative word in this thought is "*calmly.*" In my opinion, the Church is the ultimate example of this kind of calm, unwavering dedication to doing good and contributing to the prevention of evil. If you think about it, the Church refuses to fight evil head on. It refuses to even defend itself when it is slandered and attacked. Our leaders refuse to engage in any kind of retribution toward those who slander the Church. Instead, the Church (which is led by the Lord through the Prophet and the Apostles) keeps its eye single to the glory of the Lord, steadfast in its sure course.

I am so grateful every time I hear of another sister getting past Satan's efforts to engage her in a fighting spirit—even if she thinks she's fighting for her husband's very soul. It is a victory for truth every time a sister awakens to the wisdom in letting go of being her husband's conscience (remembering that is the role of Christ), and finds herself free to seek recovery for herself.

It seems so unnatural and wrong not to worry about what he's doing, not to be doing everything I can to stop him, protect him, or convince him. It seems like I am letting him get away with it if I don't do something. But, as I try it, I am learning that those feelings are not true at all. He doesn't really get away with anything.

So do I sit idly by and watch our marriage and family go down the drain? NO. What I can do is learn as much as I can and let Heavenly Father heal me by drawing closer to Him, rather than closer to an obsessive hurt, pain or fear. I have to replace all those actions, behaviors and fears with God, just as my husband has to replace his addiction with God. It seems unfair, but it is really quite equal. — *Sally*

Colleen: If You Stop Watching, He May Get Worse—for a While

It's a real possibility that if you stop monitoring his every action, he could get worse—at least for a while. Why? Because if he has been relying on your censure and blame to keep him from doing his addiction, your decision to pull out of the game may leave him without an active conscience.

On the other hand, if he has been using your censure and blame to *justify* doing his addiction, he will be left without an excuse to keep doing it. He will be left alone with his own choices as well as with the pain they cause. He will have to begin to face his addiction for himself and decide what *he's* going to do about it.

It was one of the hardest things I've ever done, but I had to learn to stop monitoring and stepping in to control my husband's choices. I had to let him come face to face with the truth of how addicted he really was and how deeply it was damaging his life. I had to let the sifting and sorting process that mortality is designed to accomplish take effect in his life. I had to have the humility to allow him to find answers on his own, through other means than myself.

> *I had to get out of the way and realize that the infidelity my husband was acting out was not toward me. Ultimately, in eternal reality, it was an issue between him and God. He is Heavenly Father's child, not mine.*   — *Patty*

This is about your husband and his relationship with God, specifically with the Lord Jesus Christ. No other degree of loyalty—even to you as his spouse—is going to give your husband the desire to turn away from the almost constant daily temptations he will face in the world we live in today. His conscience (the light of Christ) must be re-established in his heart and mind. That is not going to happen until you can be still and leave him alone with the Lord.

When You Feel Desperate to Know If He's Staying Clean

If you are supposed to find out more about your husband's progress in recovery and are willing to know the truth, you can trust the Lord that He will bring it to your knowledge without you having to act like a super sleuth. As you prayerfully consult with the Lord and pay attention to His calm, steady guidance, you will be *given* to know what you need to know and you will be *given* the strength and wisdom to act according to His Spirit.

It has been my experience that when I was led by the Lord to discover a new aspect of my husband's addiction, I was also sustained and calmed by His Spirit. I was able to respond with respect for myself and for my husband as well. There was a feeling of being solid, anchored, and at peace—even when I discovered something that once would have devastated me.

I keep having to remind myself that the Lord will let me know if things aren't right, and right now he is telling me things are right. If I let go of the fear and begin to really trust, then I will have a great deal of peace and joy. Even if the betrayal comes again, it is better to let go of the fear. If I hold on to the fear, then I am unhappy and miserable all the time in preparation for what might happen.

And what if it doesn't? What if he really has changed this time and never lies to me again? If I keep fearing and worrying, I will spend the rest of my life with an ache in my heart and hurting all the time. — Georgina

---

Phil: A Husband's Perspective

Once again, may I add my witness and echo what Colleen has said about the importance of the wife honoring her husband's agency. This is something Colleen has done a very good job with as she has dealt with my addiction. When we married, I had been attending Twelve Step meetings for less than a year, so my recovery was very new and still a little shaky. In fact, I had several slips during the first year of our marriage. It was one of the hardest things I have ever done to tell her each time I slipped.

She did not panic or go into hysterics at what I had to tell her. She reacted honestly to me, with tears and the truth about how much she was hurting over my actions. Still, she didn't attack me personally. In fact, even through her tears, she would thank me for my honesty. She never shamed me or took responsibility for my recovery. She didn't sermonize, or remind me of what I needed to do. I already knew, and she knew that I knew. That left the ball clearly in my court.

The one thing she did every time was to encourage me to return to the Lord and to keep trusting that He would continue to strengthen me. She told me she believed in me, and she "had it on the best authority" that the Lord believed in me, too. I was astounded at her trust of Him and humbled by her willingness to treat me like an adult.

The fact that she trusted me to listen to my conscience and seek healing from the Savior reassured me that she regarded me as a basically good person who had the ability to grow and learn from my mistakes. She trusted the principles in the Twelve Steps for what they are—the gospel principles of repentance. They had blessed her life, and she trusted they would bless mine.

The fact that I was working a program, attending meetings, studying the Twelve Step literature and the scriptures, and trying to counsel with and follow my Savior helped her, I am sure. But it helped her only insofar as it gave her more peace. I am certain that had I not been sincerely trying to change, her behavior toward me would not have been different, but the future of our marriage might have been—it might not have survived.

I am so grateful that the Lord blessed me with the willingness to work this program, and that He also blessed me with a wife who gave me the space and time I needed for these principles to take effect in my life.

Chapter **7** Keeping Priorities
Grounded in Truth

It is probably safe to assume that when you and your husband decided to marry, you were both physically attracted to each other, and rightfully and righteously so. Wanting each other, physically, was a powerful component in your relationship, but it probably wasn't all that either of you enjoyed about each other. When you looked into each other's eyes, you saw your future. You wondered what your children would look like. Neither of you were pretending anything.

You were, as the saying goes, "playing for keeps." You both had the same hopes, the same dreams, the same priorities and the same values— a home, a family, an eternal partnership. Now as you find that the adversary has taken your husband's heart and mind prisoner and locked him into a form of slavery—turning his own body's chemistry against him—you must not abandon those priorities and values.

Colleen: Two Ways Lust Can Drag You into Its Clutches

Dear Sister, Satan has subtle ways of whispering lust into *your* mind and heart that you must recognize and flee from, as if your very life depends on it. One is becoming obsessive about your weight. The other is becoming addicted to viewing pornography yourself.

I don't know if, in your past, you've ever been caught in the trap of obsessing about your weight, but please pray for the grace to keep you from letting your husband's addiction lure you into developing an obsessive-compulsive disorder around the subject of weight. Satan can lead you into this so subtly, disguising his intention behind your desire to be healthier. Remember that becoming healthier does *not* include such extreme measures as starving, exercising compulsively, or forcing yourself to vomit or use laxatives in order to alter your weight as quickly as possible.

Another way Satan may try to take you down into the depths of slavery is to get you hooked on pornography, right alongside your husband. This is a condition that goes beyond the occasional unexpected and abhorrent exposure to pornography, and goes beyond that one exposure that keeps tempting you to compare yourself with what you've seen.

No, I'm talking about descending to a level of lust that infects your own soul. At first, Satan will lie to you and get you to believe that you're just looking so that you can know, first-hand, what your husband has seen. But, then, a lust of your own begins to build. Either it will be a lust for what these women have that you want—a body that virtually commands your husband's attention—or an addiction to the internal chemistry created in your own body by such images.

This very dangerous situation begins when the single act (uninvited and abhorrent) begins to be tolerated and repeated. Remember the chart in Chapter One that describes the downward spiral into addiction? If you have fallen to the urge to go back and look at pornography alone, in secret, please go back and review the chart. The end stage of addiction is possession (see p. 15).

Lust and Love Are Exact Opposites

We mentioned earlier that most young men have the erroneous belief that getting married will cure their sexual addiction. Ironically, most wives think the same thing and wonder why their sexual relations aren't enough for their husbands. The lie that both of them are falling for is the lie that what sex in marriage offers and what illicit sex provides is the same thing. Nothing could be further from the truth, and it is *essential* that you understand why.

The intimate experiences a husband has with his wife are acts of *love* and not lust. It is *lust* that the man who views pornography is addicted to, that he is enslaved by. That is why it is totally possible for a man to truly be engaging in an act of love when he participates in sex with his wife, and also why that act of love does *not* satisfy his craving for a "lust-fix."

We know this is a challenging idea to grasp, but we hope that you will take it to Heavenly Father in prayer and seek His confirmation. It is such an essential truth and has the potential to heal your heart of one of the most personal lies Satan is trying to perpetrate on you.

In truth, the sex men experience "alone" or with another uncommitted partner has nothing at all to do with love. It is only lust, and lust—as crazy as it may sound—is a deficit that no amount of physical gratification can fill.

Lust is a malignant imitation of love that feeds on its host and actually creates a craving for more of itself. I know the comparison may seem too simple, but it may help to think about the difference between eating healthy foods that are filled with genuine nourishment and eating junk food that leaves your soul starving and wanting more of what does you no good, but only harm.

It Is Possible for Lust to Invade Your Intimate Relations

Unfortunately, it can happen in some cases that a man will allow lust to infect his sexual experiences with his wife. When this happens, it usually doesn't take a wife long to recognize the shift in spirit or energy during their "love-making." Feelings of mutual consideration and enjoyment begin to fade. Her sense of ease and safety with him begins to suffer as he starts asking her to participate in actions that make her feel troubled and even repulsed. Still, she may feel compelled to go along, fearing he will be hurt—maybe even angry—if she doesn't.

More than one wife has been deceived into joining her husband in sexual practices she does not feel comfortable with, including viewing pornography with him. This is another way that Satan tries to get to you. He will lie to you and tempt you to think that if you go along with your husband in viewing pornography, you can keep his attention, or at least you can know what he's doing and feel somewhat "in control."

Don't be fooled by this lie. You won't gain anything from participating, and as we mentioned earlier, you could very well become addicted to pornography yourself.

Never, never force yourself, to participate in any sexual act that you do not feel you can perform with a sincere heart and a clear conscience. You, as a woman, have every right to trust your prayerful feelings. Pray continually in your heart, in all your doings, seeking the spirit of truth to guide your thoughts and actions. The Lord has promised us that if we will do this, He will **"direct [us] for good."**[1]

In nothing do we need His counsel more than in this sacred, intimate portion of our lives. You can be sure He cares deeply about how you feel, and that He wants you to feel like the "queen of your own body," as the Prophet David O. McKay put it.

> **A woman should be queen of her own body. The marriage covenant does not give a man the right to... use her merely for the gratification of his passion** (*Conference Report,* April, 1952, 86-87).

Colleen: Never Let Your Intimacy Be Based on a Lie

When I learned of my first husband's sexual addiction and the lengths to which he had taken it, I found I could not in all honesty continue a physical relationship with him. Of course, this angered and upset him, but I felt I had to be true to the spirit of truth. Sex with him at that point would not have been an expression of a loving relationship. It would have been a deception, a travesty—in short, a lie. I expressed my feelings at the time in this poem:

Lies

You came,
Lying to me.
And I fell for it.
You wanted me to lie with you
And I did.
I lied to myself.
But I am through now.
Through
And through.
I'm through
Lying
And calling it
Love.

Fortunately, most of the men who are trapped in this awful addiction are good men who have made some foolish choices. They desperately want to get out of this mess, but cannot without Divine help. If you feel in your heart that your husband is basically a good man and that he does love you, there is no reason you cannot continue sexual relations with him as long as you feel good about it and the promptings you receive from the Spirit agree. This is a place where *your* personal revelation is the ultimate bottom line. Continuing legitimate sexual relations may serve as a striking contrast to the illegitimate imitation portrayed in pornography.

Phil: Trust Your Prayerful Feelings

You have the right to abstain from sexual contact with your husband for your own recovery reasons. You have to put your recovery first. If your personal recovery honestly requires that you abstain from sex with him, then that's the truth. You need to honor that truth. You need to realize that to be false and participate in sex when, in your deepest heart, you are really feeling used, abused, unloved, and unloving is a lie. No genuine happiness comes from living a lie.

As I have counseled with many active LDS men, I have found that they are very aware that lust is a cheap substitute for real love. They are not oblivious to the huge difference between the blessed and nurturing feelings created by the love they share with their wives and the cheapened, degraded feelings that come with illicit sex of any kind. I hope you can feel some comfort in my testimony that your husband's addiction does not automatically mean that he is practicing lust when he is intimate with you.

As Colleen has suggested, I hope you will be very prayerful about whether you should avoid intimate relations with your husband. Let the Lord guide you through the impressions and feelings that express the truth of your heart. Your feelings count. If you are prayerful, you can trust them. Let these feelings be your guide, rather than anyone else's opinions, including, and perhaps especially, your husband's.

---

1. Alma 37:37.

Section 2

Continuing in the Truth, Outliving the Lies

Chapter 8

What It Means to Be Codependent

When you try to get through your day and can barely function; when you lie down at night and can't sleep; when you wake up agonizing about your husband's choices; when no amount of counting your blessings makes any difference because *all* you crave is for him to stop practicing his addiction, then you are in the grip of an addiction-like spiral of your own which many people refer to as "codependency."

No one knows exactly where the term "codependency" began. It is thought that it was first used by someone in the addiction recovery field who was trying to name the painful, fearful, responsible way the loved ones of addicts often feel. Whatever it is called, it cannot be denied that this condition keeps you from living *your* life, having *your* opinions, learning *your* lessons, thinking *your* thoughts, and being a sovereign person in your own right. Maybe a quick way to explain it would be to say that if you were to think of the addict as someone who is drowning, the codependent is someone who is "co-drowning."

Most essentially, codependency means that your mind and heart are as hung up on your husband and his choices as his mind and heart are hung up on his addiction. Because of your deep reliance on your addicted loved one's moment-to-moment ups or downs, you are robbed of a peaceful, happy life too, just as he is! As one wife put it: "It's sort of like breathing second-hand smoke. You're not the smoker, but the quality of your life is being sacrificed by your reaction to his addiction."

Such feelings of constant preoccupation and craving for your husband's recovery could also rightfully be described as an obsession. Suffering from an obsession is like being dragged behind a galloping horse with your foot stuck in the stirrup. You can't control the horse and you can't free yourself from the punishment of bouncing along behind it. This is how an addict of any kind (including a codependent) feels toward the object of his or her addiction.

Another way to put it is that you are in bondage to your husband's bondage. His intense dependency for some form of unrighteous sexual behavior has enslaved him, making him behave in totally irrational and foolish ways. Meanwhile, you—his partner—are also struggling to avoid acting in ways that are irrational—raging at him, hating him or yourself, withdrawing from others, feeling like your whole life is a waste. Maybe you are even being tempted to blame God. No matter how many resolutions you make to yourself to stay calm and deal with this crisis in a sane way, it's as if all your good intentions fly out the window and a spirit of bitterness takes over that swamps you with feelings of regret and resentment.

Colleen: How Understanding "Codependency" Has Helped Me

Over the years since it first began to be used, the word "codependency" has been heavily debated in the professional world. I've been told more than once that it is nothing more than a buzz word, a pop-psychology term. Some people even say that it is just another negative label we wives need to feel guilty about. I disagree.

For me, seeking to understand this concept of codependency was the foundation of regaining my own sanity in the midst of the nightmarish reality that my husband's addiction created around me. If I have vertigo and can hardly function due to a loss of my sense of balance, and someone else has something that can give me significant help in dealing with it—maybe even healing it—I really don't mind what they call my problem. It only matters that their suggested treatment is restoring my ability to function in a normal manner.

I am confident that reading through this chapter and the next (which will address codependency from a gospel perspective) will give you much food for thought and prayerful reflection and insight. I believe studying about codependency will help you understand that:

1. You are not losing your mind.

2. You are not alone; others have felt this way.

3. You have been doing your best to survive your husband's addiction, and you don't have to feel ashamed or guilty that you've tried to help him.

Exposing the Two Faces of Codependency

There are actually a lot of good things we do in our lives, even *righteous* things, that if taken to an excess, cease to be good and become detrimental. Food, exercise, sleep, work, leisure—the list could go on and on. Being a loving person, full of desire to do what is right and help others do what is right, is a great strength, but like any other strength, it has the potential to go too far.

It is hard for a loving, caring person to admit that loving and caring can exceed righteous, balanced limits. When it does, genuine love has mutated into either one or the other of two forms of codependency: 1) fear *of* the addict and assuming responsibility for his moods, especially anger; or 2) fear *for* the addict, assuming responsibility for protecting and rescuing him from his addiction by controlling his choices.

This dual face of codependency is one of the reasons it is such an elusive and confusing concept to thoroughly understand. It is my prayer that you won't become discouraged in your efforts to sort it out. You can be sure we are closing in on one of Satan's most powerful strategies.

Let's take an example of another ailment that can manifest two seemingly opposite sets of symptoms—having a fever. One minute the sufferer is burning up and only a few minutes later he is displaying the opposite symptoms, shaking with chills. While it is the same underlying illness, it manifests opposite symptoms. So it is with codependency, especially in its early stages. On one hand, you feel dominated, crushed, and controlled by your husband's addiction. At this extreme, you may go for hours, days, even weeks, living in constant fear of his every mood, terrified that you might upset him and cause him to act out again. Then, almost in an instant, your response may flip to the polar opposite and you find yourself swept up in a feverish determination to save him from himself by taking over as his caretaker and his conscience.

One way or the other, whether shivering with fear or burning up with the need to take charge, you have lost your sense of sovereignty and control over your own life. You feel more like a helpless passenger in a car that is spinning on ice, first careening off one guardrail and then the other, crashing from one extreme to the other. Whichever form your codependency takes, you are still trapped in a lie that you must either live like a helpless victim to your husband's choices or that you must take on the burden of saving him from himself and his addiction.

Colleen: Feeling Dominated and Victimized

When a codependent person feels dominated or victimized, they will accept far more inappropriate behavior, especially blame and shame, from their addicted partner than would a person with a strong sense of self-worth and personal agency. This high tolerance for emotional distance and tension in her home, with or without actual verbalized rudeness, is usually learned during childhood. Over the years, the role of victim has become a way of life.

> *I'm feeling like what good is it going to do if I spend effort and time on myself, getting myself healthier, and my husband just stays where he is?* — Mia

Resorting to what is familiar, the codependent becomes the helpless one in the marriage. She goes along with the addict, afraid of making him do something more or something worse. She can't imagine living life by herself. She feels that without her husband and the dreams and expectations she has invested in him, her life would be purposeless and worthless. Many women in this mode of codependency begin to victimize themselves by neglecting their own care and improvement.

Oh, how I remember what this was like with my first husband. I was absolutely terrified of his moodiness. I was so afraid of setting him off that I would go along with just about anything.

I believed that I could love him out of his upset moods and negative thinking. I believed that if I would just do more and do better, it would be the missing link or ingredient to inspire him to be happier and more attentive and loving toward me and the children. I lived in constant fear that he didn't love me and that he might leave me—and that it all would be my fault. I was so desperate and dependent upon him loving me—or at least not leaving me—that I rationalized his every unkind, abusive, and self-centered behavior. And you better believe he loved this arrangement and encouraged me to stay in this role. I've often said that the one thing we both had most in common, even more than the Church or our children, was that we both held me accountable for everything. We were president and vice-president of the "Everything Is Colleen's Fault Club." We both believed that with all our hearts.

As I began to study recovery principles for my own sake, not to coach him or support him, I realized I had to stop obsessing about what he had or had not done, what he was or was not doing, what he might or might not do. I had to start focusing on what was going on inside of me that was keeping me fixated and dependent on living a life consumed in this much suffering. Admitting that I might actually be keeping myself in such a state of helplessness and neediness was hard, but eventually I was able to admit it without blaming or shaming myself.

Finally, I realized that there was no one holding the prison doors of pain and confusion closed except me, as I leaned against them from the inside! Could that be true? Could it really be that while my husband was addicted to sex, I was addicted to playing the "poor me" role of a victim? Recovery for me began when I faced the truth that there was something in my own character—a belief that I had formed somewhere in my life's journey—that Satan was counting on me to keep believing. This was what I needed the Savior's help to recover from!

I recognize that I was codependent before I was married. For as long as I can remember I have been fearful of what others thought of me. I've needed to have some sort of relationship or connection to someone else in order to feel any value or worth. I always had to look and appear perfect. I can look at anybody else and see plainly why God loves them, but I have never been able to see that for myself. I have always felt defective or worthless for some reason. I thought marriage would fill the void that I felt in my life. Unfortunately it just made things ten times worse in some areas, but strangely, I feel a lot of growth in other areas. Anyway this is a new revelation to me about myself. — Kayann

---

Colleen: Feeling the Need to Inspire and Save Him

While the "victim mode" of codependency is the one I spent most of my time locked into, I have to admit that I did my fair share of thinking in the "Savior mode" as well. In this mode, it was almost like going into a bipolar manic phase of being. Instead of acting depressed and dominated, I would take exactly the opposite attitude. I would become very pro-active, trying to control my husband and save him from his own choices, no matter how he responded. All that mattered is that someone take control of the situation, and if he wouldn't do it, then obviously, I had to.

In this state of mind, I was determined to be my husband's savior. I was going to be his bright and shining star. I was going to play his conscience and his inspiration. Surely, I thought, this is what being a "helpmeet" means. After all, I had heard many a good man say that his wife was the light of his life and his better half. I was determined to shoulder the responsibility, to give my very life if necessary, in order to keep everything in our home wonderful and thus make certain my husband stayed clean and sober of sexual sin.

When I thought I was connecting with my husband, I was really just connecting with what I wanted him to be. I was so obsessed with him that I couldn't see what I was doing.... I was hurting or that he was hurting. I believed in my heart that love conquered all—that if I loved him harder, longer, stronger, if I sacrificed more, and made him understand, then we would have the most beautiful love.   — Angela

---

Colleen: Letting Go of the "Savior" Role

So much of my self-worth and pride were invested in believing that I, Mother, was the heart of the home and that I, Mother, was powerful enough to set the mood in my home. I interpreted those statements to mean that somehow I must be the person with ultimate responsibility, ultimate authority, and ultimate power in our home. It has taken a very long time to let go of the shame and blame and disgust I felt toward myself for failing at wielding that power successfully.

It was not until I humbled myself and admitted the limits of my own humanity by prayerful study and personal application of the principles in the Twelve Step program that peace began to replace my often hysterical feelings and behaviors. By taking each step as a true principle that could help me put my role in correct perspective, I began to seek Christ personally and singularly to "set the mood" in my heart.

As I made the Savior the person who was the heart of my life, I was able to surrender to Him the burden of "savior-ship" I had previously assumed toward my husband. Laying that burden at His feet and seeking His counsel and comfort, I felt His testimony that He was the *only* person with the power to change my loved ones' hearts. I realized that there is only one soul that I have ultimate stewardship over—my own. If I were going to be an influence for good to my husband and children, my source of hope had to shift from my own feeble, mortal efforts and move toward hope in the Lord Jesus Christ and His power to redeem and heal me. I had to get out of the "savior" role and let the Savior take over, starting with me.

The Best Way to Help Your Husband: Detach with Love

We testify, again, that as paradoxical as it may sound, the most important thing you can do for your husband is to "detach with love" from him and let him take the responsibility for his own recovery. You must accept the fact that just as you did not cause his addiction, nothing you do can cure it.

Your husband needs to hear you admit the truth that there's nothing you can do to keep him from acting out. He needs to hear you confess that you are relying on the Savior for the strength to get through each day, just as much as he is. He needs to hear you testify that your commitment to remaining with him is the result of the Savior's witness to you of *His* faith in *both* of you and in your marriage.

When I first heard the phrase "detach with love" offered as the way out of codependency, I thought, "What in the world could 'detach with love' mean? You don't *detach* from someone if you love them!" Could it really ever be righteous to detach? Is it ever charitable?

In answer to that question directed to the Lord, He brought a story to my remembrance that I had heard a speaker tell many years before. The story was about a nearly tragic rafting accident in which he and his daughter were thrown out of their raft when it hit a submerged rock and tipped. It has become a powerful parable to me in my healing from codependency. I recognized it was the perfect parable to convey how "detaching" can be an act of love—in fact it *can* be an act of God.

Swim for Shore: A Powerful Parable

The speaker began his story describing a family vacation and the high adventure of spending a day on a white-water river-rafting trip.

Most of the course of the swift river was smooth and invigorating, surrounded as they were by exquisite mountain scenery. There would be some stretches of rapids, though, and the anticipation of riding through them was a big part of the thrill of the day.

As the raft filled with excited adventurers was carried along on the current, it became obvious that the streambed beneath was growing rockier. Boulders could be seen just below the surface that caused the current to pass over them in smooth, unbroken humps of icy water. The river guide was doing his best to avoid these hidden obstacles, but suddenly the edge of the raft was caught in the upward rise of water over a boulder and the raft bucked and nearly flipped.

In a split second, the fun of running the river turned to terror for this father and his daughter as they both were thrown from the raft and into the frigid temperatures of the river. Even though they were wearing life jackets, the deep current around the rocks pulled them under and the shock of the cold water was immediate. Dazed and confused, father and daughter began to desperately flail around, grabbing at each other. Their frantic efforts only served to submerge them both over and over again.

Gasping for breath, the father realized he and his child were being swept away from the raft and ever closer to the actual rapids. Terror set in as he realized they could die in this incident. "O God," he cried out. "Please let me save my child. Please!"

Into his mind came the most irrational and counter-intuitive thought: "Turn and swim for shore."

He couldn't believe that thought could be from God! How could God tell him to turn away from his child and swim for his life. He knew he could probably make it on his own, but he couldn't just abandon her to be pulled under and swept away, possibly to her death!

In a growing panic, he kept trying to get a hold on her, but with no lasting success. He could feel his strength waning. He knew that within a very short period of time he wouldn't have the strength to even save himself. They would both be lost.

"Swim for shore." The words came to his mind again. Finally a third time. "Swim for shore!" He could no longer deny the clarity and the finality in the words. They were a command.

Feeling like a failure, feeling he had lost his daughter, feeling he was saving himself while leaving her to drown, he turned sobbing and swam diagonally across the powerful current toward the shoreline. He couldn't believe how strong the current was. Every stroke felt like his last. He felt like he weighed a thousand pounds and even when he his feet touched bottom near the shore, he couldn't keep his balance and had to keep swimming.

Finally, after what seemed like forever, he found himself in shallow water moving slow enough that he could get his feet under him. Only then, when he tried to stand up, did he realize that what he had thought was the terrible grasp of the swift current pulling him backwards was actually the weight of his daughter who had grabbed hold of a dangling strap on the back of his life jacket. Thus, in obeying the impressions of the Spirit to swim for shore, he had not only saved himself, but his child as well.

As I sat there that day, listening to this story, I cried. I knew it was the Spirit of Truth bearing down upon my soul in personal witness. This was what I needed to do, too, in trying to save my loved one. I needed to listen to the Spirit and follow the impressions the Lord whispered to my mind. I couldn't go on doing what I was doing, which was flailing around in my attempts to save my loved one from the treacherous rapids of addiction. Like this father, I was in despair, because it seemed like all my attempts to reach my loved one only seemed to push him further from me. I had to swim for shore myself.

Turning to the Scriptures for Understanding of Codependency

Even after I felt the Spirit confirm the truth of this parable to my personal situation, there was still the question in my mind of how I could *know* the Spirit's voice from all the other voices and trains of thought running through my mind? There were new books constantly coming out, telling me the latest techniques and approaches to dealing with an addicted loved one. I truly felt like someone caught in the **"Lo here! Lo there!"**[1] dilemma that the Prophet Joseph Smith described when considering the religious traditions and persuasions in his day. Which of all of them was right? Desperately, I looked for one approach that would have all the answers I needed in the trenches, as the saying goes—in the day-to-day interactions with my addicted loved one. I needed to have these new ideas grounded in Christ.

As I studied the Book of Mormon, seeking validation for each of the Twelve Steps, I began to see something I had never seen before. I began to hear its witness of the absolute need I had for a Savior, every bit as much as my husband did. I began to awaken to the fact that Jesus was the Holy *One* of Israel, and the *only* person commissioned and sent by our Father in Heaven to save us—to save me! He was the shore. He was the sure foundation. He was the rock, the source of all the revelation I needed to counsel and comfort me in every area of my life. Only then could I face the awful spiritual hurricanes and tornadoes—the very whirlwinds the prophets had foretold—that were ripping every traditional value and cultural standard apart. Only by coming to Him to save my own life, could I offer anyone else hope of rescue or recovery from the addictive behaviors the world portrayed as "fun."

Attempting to change negative behaviors by grabbing at our loved ones when we too are in water over our heads is like the father and daughter pulling each other down. We can never get our loved ones to quit doing what they're doing by coming at them head on. The only effective long-term solution is to help them come to Christ by doing it for ourselves. We cannot be agents of peace unless we have peace in our own hearts. Only internal peace can make us peacemakers.

Love alone brings this peace—the **"pure love of Christ"**[2] kind of love. A person who loves the Lord above all others and knows the sweetness of His love in return will learn directly from Him how to have a **"peaceable walk with the children of men."**[3]

As a practicing, believing LDS woman, I needed to see these ideas anchored in the teachings of the prophets. Once again, I turned to the scriptures to either validate these ideas or refute them. You can only imagine my surprise when I found that, even though the word itself was not found in the scriptures, the confusion of boundaries and the self-seeking disguised as service to others could be seen in every standard work. In the next chapter, I have offered some of the personal insights I gained as I studied. I hope they may help you also see the spiritual roots of this subtle and cunning counterfeit of Godly love.

1. Pearl of Great Price, Joseph Smith–History 1:5.

2. Moroni 7:47.

3. Moroni 7:4.

Chapter 9 — Codependency: A Gospel Perspective

There are two species of snakes that look so much alike that it takes an expert eye to tell them apart. The bite of one is deadly; the other is harmless. One is the coral snake, whose venom is extremely lethal, second only to rattlesnake venom. The other is the equally bright colored, but totally benign milk snake. Their nearly identical appearance makes it a matter of life or death to be absolutely certain which one you are dealing with. So it is with codependency and charity.

Though actions motivated by codependency may look like charity on the surface, it is what lies beneath the surface that matters most. It is the motivation found in the invisible realm of one's *real* intent and in the spirit prompting the behavior that makes the difference.

Charity relies on the Savior's guidance to administer love in healthy ways. Codependency is absolutely poisonous to one's spiritual life as well as to the person receiving help. Charity fosters a sense of faith and hope for both giver and receiver.[1] Codependent relationships drain both people of hope and faith. When acting with charity, under Christ's pure love and influence, both parties feel mutually edified. Codependent behavior leaves both parties feeling used and manipulated.

Codependency Always Has a Price Tag

Codependency *always* has a price tag; it always expects something in return for the "love" it gives. Codependent acts are never freely given.

They may look generous and self-sacrificing on the outside, but they are a form of manipulation to get a desired result. Codependency gives service so that it may require service—an effective way to put the recipient of that service in bondage.

Charity, in complete contrast to codependency, **"seeketh not her own."**[2] In other words, charity does not come with a price tag and it doesn't have expectations. Instead, charity encourages hope and faith. It is the kind of love that God feels towards us even if we refuse to cooperate with His desire to rescue us from our unwise and unrighteous choices. You can see God's love and charity in the fact that no matter how far we wander, He will never be the one to give up His effort to forgive and redeem us:

> **Yea, and as often as my people repent will I forgive them their trespasses against me (Mosiah 26:30).**

> **Behold, ye are little children and ye cannot bear all things now; ye must grow in grace and in the knowledge of the truth.**

> **Fear not, little children, for you are mine, and I have overcome the world, and you are of them that my Father hath given me;**

> **And none of them that my Father hath given me shall be lost (Doctrine & Covenants 50:40-42; emphasis added).**

Colleen: The Difference Between Expectations and Hope

I'll never forget my surprise when the Lord presented me with the thought: "Colleen, you need to know that expectations are actually *premeditated* resentments." At first I was puzzled. What? Premeditated? As in, planning on something or setting it up ahead of time?

Suddenly, I saw the truth of it. I set myself up to be hurt and disappointed when I *expect* something and it doesn't come through. What should I do if I can't expect something from myself or my loved one? I posed my question to the Lord. The answer came with such meekness and mildness: You can have *hope*.

I felt puzzled again, but I was willing to sit still and ponder these ideas for a while. As I did, I began to *feel* the difference. When I *hope* something for someone else or for myself, there is a lighter, gentler feeling in my heart for them and toward them. I don't feel like I'm going to be personally let down if what I hope for doesn't come through. By contrast, when I *expect* someone to do something and they don't meet my expectations, I feel a much heavier, let down, upset feeling.

Since that day, I have applied this "paradigm shift" to my relationships. For example, I don't expect Phil to call me at lunchtime, every day, but I hope he will. If I expect it, I am much more invested in the outcome. I want to control the outcome—I want "it" to turn out according to my expectations, or else! Or else what? Or else I will be sad, upset, offended, hurt—maybe even outright angry. But hope sits lightly on my heart and leaves me to accept the situation as it comes to pass and allows me the freedom to let go and to move on to hope again.

One of the most powerful demonstrations of charity and its fostering of hope came into my life as I watched the relationship between my husband Phil and his first wife Kathy in the last months before she passed away. Watching Phil's tenderness toward Kathy, even though her health had taken an irreversible downward turn that limited their hope for a larger family and a long life together, taught me first-hand what it means to live with the gracious relinquishment of hope.

Watching Kathy's kindness toward Phil, even when he confessed his ongoing struggle with pornography, was a living demonstration to me that genuine love isn't something you give only if your spouse earns it by living up to *your* expectations or making sure *your* dreams are fulfilled. I felt no resentment in either of them towards life or towards God for dreams that were obviously not going to come to pass. I cannot sufficiently express my gratitude for being allowed to witness a marriage based on the foundation of charity that they forged in their twenty-eight years together.

Practicing the Second Commandment As It Is Written

I have heard it taught that I should divide my love up into three portions and put them in this order: First, love of God; second, love of others; and third, love of myself. As I listen carefully, though, and slowly ponder the Savior's words, I feel His testimony to my heart that there are really only two levels of love mentioned there, not three.

> **Master, which is the great commandment in the law?**
>
> **Jesus said unto him, Thou shalt love the Lord thy God with all thy heart, and with all thy soul, and with all thy mind.**
>
> **This is the first and great commandment.**
>
> **And the second is like unto it, Thou shalt love thy neighbour as thyself.**
>
> **On these two commandments hang all the law and the prophets (Matthew 22:36-40).**

Read Mark's rendition of the same statement by the Lord:

> **And thou shalt love the Lord thy God with all thy heart, and with all thy soul, and with all thy mind, and with all thy strength: this is the first commandment.**
>
> **And the second is like, namely this, Thou shalt love thy neighbour as thyself. There is none other commandment greater than these (Mark 12:30-31).**

While I most definitely hear Him saying that I should love God above all else, I do not hear Him teaching that I should love others above myself or myself above others. For me, recovery from codependency most definitely includes remembering to keep my love of others and my love of myself equal and fairly balanced.

Turning to the Savior, seeking His counsel, I began to see that He loves me and my loved ones with exactly the same tender, patient, long-suffering love. There are times when He leads me to put my loved one's best interest first, but there are also times when it is His direct counsel to take care of my own needs first.

As I heeded the counsel of President Ezra Taft Benson, to put God ahead of *everyone* else in my life, I found the Lord blessing me with the gift of His perfect love for both me and my loved one.

> **When we put God first, all other things fall into their proper place or drop out of our lives. Our love of the Lord will govern the claims for our affection, the demands on our time, the interests we pursue, and the order of our priorities.**
>
> **We should put God ahead of *everyone* else in our lives (President Ezra Taft Benson, *Ensign*, May 1988, 4; emphasis in original).**

I can never share President Benson's statement without noting that he delivered these words in General Conference, speaking to us as *the* prophet, and that *he* was the one who had the word *"everyone"* italicized when his talk was printed in the *Ensign*.

I don't know about you, but when the prophet of the Lord puts that kind of emphasis on an idea, I listen. Put God ahead of *everyone* else in your life and everything else will "fall into its proper place."

I trusted those words. I stopped being codependent on my addicted loved ones. I stopped fearing them and I stopped fearing for them. As I practiced this principle, things began to fall into their proper place, and some things did fall out of my life entirely. I can't pretend to you that it wasn't excruciatingly painful to let go of my efforts to make everything turn out according to my definition of "right," and to let God's higher way—the way of agency—take its course. Neither can I pretend it happened overnight. It takes a lot of practice of this true principle to overcome the natural man's urge to take control.

This is why my prayer is that you will begin today to do as Moroni invited, to **"seek this Jesus."**[3] By putting Him first, He can and will direct us for good. He will teach us all things that we should do to show mutual respect and consideration for ourselves, as well as for others.

> *I am turning this over to the Lord and finding hope in Him that my relationships and desire to serve others will balance out. He is taking me through experiences that are proving my codependence and showing me how I can come to Him first and know His opinion, then take what I like and leave the rest. It is still an imperfect practice at best, but coming to know how Jesus feels about things is worth it.* — Candice

Accessing the Savior's Atonement Through The Twelve Steps

Possessing the ability to love both ourselves and others in harmony with Christ's perfect love is an effect of absorbing His character from His offer of at-one-ment with us. We develop it over time by seeking greater consciousness of His Spirit abiding with us and as we seek His counsel in all our doings.

This gift of Christ-guided love is not something we just ask for and receive. It comes as a result of allowing Him into our lives every hour. Neither is this gift accessed by "act as if" behavior. Despite all the injunctions to be Christ-like, I could never sustain the goal of being *like* Him. Rather, I had to stop *trying* so hard to be like Him, and instead relax into **"the arms of [His] love."**[5] Like the poem, "The Touch of the Master's Hand," despite the increased value the auctioneer attributed to the violin, it was the Master, not the violin, who made the difference. Just as the old violin can do nothing more than the one who possesses it, neither can my heart and mind know how to love *like* Christ—but only as I am *as one* with Him.

Abide in me, and I in you. As the branch cannot bear fruit of itself, except it abide in the vine; no more can ye, except ye abide in me. I am the vine, ye are the

branches: He that abideth in me, and I in him, the same bringeth forth much fruit: for without me ye can do nothing (John 15:4-5).

Learning to trust Christ's offer of at-one-ment with us happens gradually, with quite a few ebbs and flows, slips and recommitments. Just like the addict who is willing to humbly persist at his recovery, we family members must be willing to accept that coming unto Christ is a process. We must accept the reality that as long as we are mortal, the natural man in us will resist charity, just like our husbands will have to surrender to a life-long inclination to resist abstinence from their addiction.

I haven't wanted to admit that I have as many things to work on as my husband—number one is my self-righteousness. I've proudly and erringly thought I didn't need to be saved quite as much as other people. I am grateful that He is letting me find peace in His love, when for so long I've been pretending to be above needing Him and His atonement. It is my prayer that I will keep feeling after the Savior with a much more humble heart—continuing to work on my own behaviors with His love and guidance—and allowing others the same freedom. — Tia

---

Here again, we find in *our Savior's communion with us* an empathy and understanding for our mutual battle against the temptations of our common enemy. Begin with charity for each other that grows from seeking the Savior's Spirit. Together, seek and accept His gracious offer of grace (power) to be at-one with Him. You can be certain that all is well and all will yet be even better in your lives and in your life together. Christ is your most important marriage partner—He is the core of our deliverance from the lies that fuel both addiction and codependency.

Pray unto the Father with all the energy of heart, that ye may be filled with this love, which *he hath bestowed*

upon all who are true followers of his Son, Jesus Christ; that ye may become the sons of God; that when he shall appear we shall be like him...that we may have this hope; that we may be purified even as he is pure. Amen (Moroni 7:48, emphasis added).

It was not until I began to study and apply the Twelve Steps for myself that I was able to access the miracle of feeling the peace of Christ and His mutual love for both me and my husband. As I said earlier, this has not been an overnight change. Still, I continue to feel myself growing in patience and love, albeit ever so gradually, as I do not give up on myself and keep coming unto Christ.[5]

I've come to realize that Jesus is always ready to help me change my perceptions to match His wisdom. He never forces or pushes me. He will not take away my agency nor steal my personality. He will not force me to love Him. He does not want power over me. He wants to share His wisdom. I cannot comprehend the extent of His charity and that He wants us to learn to be as charitable as He is. — Helen

Colleen: Admitting My Need for Jesus

Before I could begin to experience charity, I had to stop acting "as if." I had to stop pretending I could manufacture a miracle if I just tried hard enough. I had to do the equivalent of taking Step One in the Twelve Steps: I had to admit that as the *child* of God that I am, I don't have the capacity to even grasp what it means to love like God. I am as far from that as a kindergartner is from a PhD in nuclear physics.

All I can do to obtain this gift of God's love for my husband is to keep coming to the Lord and sharing all my own imperfect, fear-infected efforts to love with Him. I need the Savior Jesus Christ to pick me up in

His adult arms and wrap me around in His fully mature, developed degree of righteousness and purity. I cannot drum up perfect love, no matter how hard I try. Perfect love is what God has; it is what God has become. When I humble myself before Him and explain my real feelings, I find that He accepts my confession of honest weakness and covers it in His strength. He does not reject me for my imperfect way of thinking and feeling. Instead He takes my weakness and replaces it with His love for myself and my husband in equal measure.

Colleen: Seeing Codependency as the Opposite of God's Love

Across all the literature I've read on codependency, both as a code-pendent myself and as a doctoral student in human development, I have found repeated references to the idea that codependency is the result of a person (or a group of people, such as a family) not knowing how to set and maintain healthy personal boundaries, not knowing how to individ-uate or to establish personal autonomy.

Once again, wanting to be sure that what I was being taught in school squared with the scriptures, I went searching for these ideas. I was sure I wouldn't find the exact words, but what, I wondered, might be the scriptural equivalent? Two words whispered through my mind: *agency* and *stewardship*. Further investigation into scriptures dealing with these concepts eventually led me to understand the reason code-pendency has no foundation in the principles of truth.

One day as I was following the references in the Topical Guide on both of these words, I found that the first few verses of **Alma 29** were extremely insightful. I was led to read **Alma 29:1-4** with new eyes and ears. Oh my goodness! Here—at least in verses 1 and 2—I found the great prophet Alma confessing feelings that certainly paralleled my own about getting other people to repent and come unto God. Surely, no one would accuse Alma of being "codependent"?

O that I were an angel, and could have the wish of mine heart, that I might go forth and speak with the

> trump of God, with a voice to shake the earth, and cry
> repentance unto every people!
>
> Yea, I would declare unto every soul, as with the voice
> of thunder, repentance and the plan of redemption,
> that they should repent and come unto our God, that
> there might not be more sorrow upon all the face of
> the earth (Alma 29:1-2).

How I identified with Alma's longing. I too wished that I could have that kind of influence to cry repentance! And hey, I'd settle for just my own family. I'd settle for just my addicted husband. If I could only do or say something—*anything*—that would ensure his repentance and get him to see the light and forsake his sin. How could that be anything but a *righteous* desire on my part? But then I read:

> But behold, I am a man, and do sin in my wish; for I
> ought to be content with the things which the Lord
> hath allotted unto me (Alma 29:3).

What? Alma! How could you say that? That you sin in your wish? How could it be that you and I **"do sin in [our] wish"** that we could get someone else to repent and come to God?

I turned to the Lord and felt Him invite me to receive and record His counsel to me through Alma's continued testimony. Humbly, I offer the following thoughts, as they counseled me and straitened me (straightened out my understanding) concerning the sacred nature of agency:

> I ought not to harrow up in my desires, the firm
> decree of a just God. (*Colleen, in your obsession to see
> your loved one repent, you are actually trying to harrow up
> or break apart My own decree which ensures his freedom to
> choose for himself.*)
>
> For I know that he granteth unto men according to
> their desire, whether it be unto death or unto life.

(Colleen, you must come to peace, even as did Alma, with the fact that every person of accountable age must be allowed to choose according to his or her own desire, to either live in a way that increases joy or in a way that brings him or her into a state of spiritual [and possibly even physical] death.)

Yea, I know that he allotteth unto men, yea, decreeth unto them decrees which are unalterable, according to their wills, whether they be unto salvation or unto destruction (Alma 29:4). *(Colleen, this "decree" is the eternally immutable principle of agency. It is unalterable— untouchable by anyone except the person himself. Only "according to their wills," can any genuine change be brought to pass in a person's life. Whether a person's choices lead them into salvation or into destruction, I, the Lord God—just like you, my child—must stand by and allow him or her that freedom. All cooperation with the principles of truth and righteousness must be voluntary or it is void and without meaning.)*

I was dumbfounded. Surely I must not have perceived that thought correctly: that even *God* is bound by these "unalterable decrees." After all, He is God, and God can do anything He wants. Right?

I didn't have to wait long for the Lord to lead me to scriptures that answered my questions and gave me a new awareness of how much God Himself honors the principle of agency. Then the eyes of my understanding were opened and I saw the truth, as I heard the following words in my mind, as if spoken by God Himself:

No power or influence can or ought to be maintained by virtue of the priesthood [or even by anyone who holds that priesthood, no matter how far they may be in eternal progression], **only by persuasion, by long-suffering, by gentleness and meekness...(Doctrine & Covenants 121:41).**

And again I had to stop Him and say, "What? Wait a minute, this sounds like it is saying that no power or influence can be maintained… even by Thee, except by persuasion, gentleness, meekness?

And as I sat, astounded, I "heard" His answer and I understood why it is so meek, and why the hymn contains the words, "How gentle God's commands."[6] *(Yes, Colleen. You now know why I seem to be so uninvolved in the affairs of men, why I don't just make them see the light and live the truth. I can't give anyone more light and truth, or grace and power than they will allow.)*

Suddenly another scripture I had recently read came into my mind, this time from the **Pearl of Great Price, Moses 7**. Here, a scene is described that I had never understood before. In these verses, Enoch has seen a vision of **"all the nations of the earth"** (v. 23), and as he did, he saw God weeping. Like me with all my questions, Enoch asked a very human, very down to earth question himself. He said to God, **"How is it that thou canst weep, seeing thou art holy, and from all eternity to all eternity?"** (v. 29) Then, Enoch goes on for two more verses rehearsing the scope and depth and height of God's power and influence and ends repeating his question, **"How is it thou canst weep?"** (v. 31)

With new ears and with an empathy for God that I would never in a million years have thought possible, I heard God's answer in **verses 32-40**, summarized in one sentence in my mind: *I weep for my children who will not choose to join me in eternal life, but instead choose the way of suffering and death.*

I knew what I had never before supposed: Even God must wait upon the ones He loves. Even He has had to learn to detach and to practice patience and faith in the face of His children's rejection of His ways. He has learned to go on with His own life and His own stewardship.

Apparently learning to detach in love, learning how to do what is best for the other person, even when it breaks one's own heart, is all part of growing into the degree of pure love God has learned to have. I am humbled to think that I could never comprehend how many times He has had to endure the risk that is always involved in loving someone else—the risk that we may have to suffer for their choices.

Personal Revelation Is the Only Antidote for Codependency

I hope that by sharing the manner in which the Lord led me to understand our Heavenly Father's unwavering respect for our agency, I may have encouraged you in two ways. First, I hope it may have helped you to catch a glimpse of how *human* our Father in Heaven really is. Exalted, it is true. Perfect, yes. But not beyond empathizing with us in our grief and heartbreak for a loved one who chooses not to follow the Way, the Truth and the Life revealed in the gospel of Christ.

Second, I hope you are beginning to realize that you are—just like I am—a regular member of the Church with plenty of imperfections not yet overcome. Even so, you can prayerfully search the scriptures and have them open up to your mind and heart, to a dialogue or conversation with the Spirit of the Lord.

I testify to you from the depths of twenty years of counseling with the Lord in this way, that the scriptures really are the *living* word of God. They will not only teach you principles of mortal human relationships, but also confirm to you the principles that guide human relationships throughout eternity. I testify to you that if you will put your relationship with God ahead of every other relationship in your life, you will find the guidance and strength to deal with your husband's recovery process and with his decision of whether or not he will turn to the Lord and choose salvation rather than destruction.

It is my testimony to you that if you will counsel with the Lord, you will know how to behave yourself toward your loved one. You will know the best thing to do, the best way to react—because you will be looking to God for your direction and not just trying to guess what to do.

And now, [my dear sisters], remember, remember that it is upon the rock of our Redeemer, who is Christ, the Son of God, that ye must build your foundation;

that when the devil shall send forth his mighty winds, yea, his shafts in the whirlwind, yea, when all his hail and his mighty storm shall beat upon you, it shall have no power over you to drag you down to the gulf of misery and endless wo, because of the rock [of revelation] upon which ye are built, which is a sure foundation, a foundation whereon if [a woman builds, she] cannot fall (Helaman 5:12, likening added).

In Conclusion

It has been years now since the knowledge of my first husband's sexual addiction swept away my earlier belief that I could rely on him—or on anyone other than the Savior—for salvation. Though at the time it often felt like I was going through open heart surgery without anesthetic, I cannot testify enough of what a blessing that "mighty change" has been in my life. Since that experience taught me how close and available my Savior and Heavenly Father are to me, Satan has lost the ability to make me feel alone in any challenge in my life. As the subsequent years have passed, I have always known that the bottom line for me when it comes to seeking advice or counsel is to "counsel with the Lord in all [my] doings."[7] I know that as I do my imperfect but willing best to look to Him, He will direct me for good, watch over me in my sleep, and give me reason to rise up in the morning grateful, no matter what challenge I may face.

1. Moroni 7:40-48.

2. 1 Corinthians 13:5.

3. Ether 12:41.

4. D&C 6:36.

5. Moroni 10:32-33.

6. Hymns, 1985, #125.

7. Alma 37:37.

10 *Living in the Light of Truth*

Lying is part of the disease of addiction—no matter what form the addiction takes. Compulsive spenders lie about their spending. Food addicts lie about their eating. Anger addicts live in denial about how often they get angry or how much it hurts others. The spiritual influence that results in addiction is a lying spirit that finds access to our minds through various means. To ignore this spiritual component of addiction is to ignore the reality that gives addiction a life of its own. Like any contagion or parasite, the lying spirits that fuel addiction's illness want to protect themselves and to maintain the secrecy that isolates the addict. This fact has been acknowledged in Twelve Step recovery by the adage: *You are only as sick as your secrets.*

As always, we can look to the teachings of the Restoration to understand the inner or spiritual life. We are taught that all of us, without exception, are beings of spirit, or in other words, we are beings of light and truth.[1] Knowing this, it is not hard to understand why living a lie would make us sick. Our spirits are nourished by truth, but they are poisoned by untruth—whether spoken aloud or kept hidden in secret.

Colleen: Without Honesty There Is No Marriage

Although honesty hurts, it is vital that we not retreat from it. I heard someone once say, "The truth will set you free, but first it will make you mad." I'm not sure about "mad," but I am sure, as the loved one of an addict, the truth will most certainly first make you cry.

I am reminded of a situation that happened with one of my children many years ago that feels like the perfect comparison or metaphor for this idea that truth sometimes has to hurt—and often over and over again—before it can heal.

One day, my ten year old daughter was helping me fix dinner. It was something she did on a regular basis and I wasn't worried for her safety. But this day there was an accident. As she reached to move a pan we had been cooking french fries in, the old handle twisted slightly. Alarmed, she forgot to let go of the pan as she jumped back from the stove. The hot oil splashed on to one of her bare legs.

Instantly, she had blisters that were already broken and weeping by the time I got her to the bathtub and started running cold water on them. One of my other children called 911, and my daughter and I rode to the hospital in an ambulance. At the hospital the doctor and nurses worked as quickly as possible to clean the wounds.

As you might imagine, we had several hard weeks as she recovered from those burns. Eventually they healed with hardly a scar, but only because for weeks my little girl had to go have the doctor snip away the thickened, lumpy skin (often called "proud flesh") that kept forming around the wounds. Every time I took her back to the doctor both of us cried, but it had to be done because that was the only way for her to heal completely with the least amount of scarring.

Thus it is with healing from an addiction, for both the addict and their loved one. They both have to be willing to go through the painful experience of telling their truth and listening to their spouse's truth. Otherwise, what they are experiencing with each other might be many things, but it will not be a genuine marriage, a genuine coming together of souls. Marriage is a far more sacred word than we can comprehend. It is a synonym for "union." It could rightfully be said marriage is even a synonym for "at-one-ment."

As Phil was going through those first slippery years of recovery, I had to accept the unavoidable truth that if either of us refused to hear the other's honest sharing, we weren't really experiencing a true marriage. How could I say something so extreme? Because a genuine marriage is based on revealing ourselves—our whole selves, imperfections and all— to each other. Without such honesty there is no true intimacy; there is no genuine, honest-to-goodness and honest-to-God marriage.

I look back now and realize that the crisis of facing Phil's addiction to pornography, which he first disclosed to me during our engagement, was the turning point that demanded we either become totally honest with each other or end our relationship. We had to sit still and face both of our realities, weaknesses and all.

I had to be willing to hear him talk about what was really going on with him, including how far his addiction had progressed. He had to be willing to listen to me tell him the truth about how much it upset me. And he did. He listened. And I did. I listened. And we both ended up comprehending each other's reality. The truth melted and melded our hearts together.

Neither of us was perfect, but we loved each other even so. We refused to fall for the adversary's efforts to make us terminally offended at each other. The truth we shared invited the Spirit of Truth to encircle us in His love for each of us. It is the same to this day, eleven years into our marriage. It has remained a genuine marriage, full of honest imperfections, but also full of honest (not fairy-tale) love.

I feel in my heart that the lying is harder to deal with than the act. I had a good talk with my husband this morning. It was hard and rather uncomfortable for both of us, but it was necessary.   *— Jill*

Don't Pretend All Is Well When It Isn't

We don't talk about it. I tried to open a dialog when I discovered his addiction, but we have said nothing about it in the last nine months. He doesn't talk, and I don't ask. We pretend there is nothing to talk about, and my husband lives with a tremendous amount of guilt every day. I believe it is affecting him physically. — April

It is easy for us, as wives of sexually addicted men, to see how sick our husbands' secrets have made them. What is sometimes more difficult to see is that we are just as likely to become spiritually, emotionally, *and* physically ill by any truth we're trying to suppress. As Phil and I have said before, the reality of your husband's sexual addiction can't be ignored without devastating consequences, any more than you could ignore the news that he has contracted any other serious physical disease. It is the same for us wives, when we try to ignore the impact of our husband's addiction on our lives. Our emotional and spiritual injuries are just as real and just as serious as are a broken limb or a bout of pneumonia.

The effort to avoid the truth and pretend that everything is fine sets you up to develop such things as depression, anxiety disorders, eating disorders and sleep disorders, just to name a few. Think of it as breathing second-hand smoke. Whether your husband owns the truth that will heal *him* or not, you must admit *your* truth to yourself and to God. You must also find a way to talk about it in an appropriate setting. You must admit your pain, your confusion, your sorrow, your fear, your regrets, and your resentments, just as you must admit, acknowledge, and lay bare a physical wound to be healed.

Pretending you don't hurt so bad that you can hardly function is a lie, an untruth. Living an untruth, living in denial, will block the Spirit of the Lord from being able to administer peace to your soul or to give counsel to you when you need it most.

After the initial shock, I realized that this reality was a part of my God-allowed package of challenges in this life. I would have to live with this reality, one way or the other—either with my husband or without him. But there was no going back and making it un-happen. — Susanne

---

Finding the Right Time and Place to Share Your Truth

Almost without exception, a wife's initial reaction to learning of her husband's sexual addiction, or upon hearing that he has slipped *yet again*, is to go into a state of shock that might last anywhere from a few minutes to a few months. Sooner or later, though, when the shock wears off, the emotions that need to be acknowledged will likely run the gamut from rage to despair and back again.

These feelings are not a sign of your lack of faith or courage. They are normal, just as normal as it would be to cry out in pain if someone suddenly backed over you with a truck and broke both your legs. No one would expect you to be still and smile through that. No one in tune with the Spirit of the Lord is going to expect you to smile and absorb the pain caused by either the initial disclosure of your husband's addiction or during the several months (or maybe even years) that it may take for your husband to find continuous deliverance from it. Still when these times come, it is important that you cry out to the Lord *first*, in that moment of pain, so that He can strengthen you and give you clarity and courage to find the right time, place, and way to speak your truth.

Admittedly, biding your time in this manner will take a super-human effort, but if you will turn to the Lord and seek His direction and His Spirit, He will bless you with the power to stay calm until you can make arrangements to discuss these things with total candor. You may want to include an understanding third party such as a priesthood leader or professional counselor on one or more of these occasions.

Finding this super-human strength to face life's challenges is what recovery means. It does not mean that pains will not come into your life. It means that when they do come, you will feel as the Psalmist wrote— that the Lord is your first resort, your source of greatest strength:

> **I will love thee, O Lord, my strength. The Lord is my rock, and my fortress, and my deliverer; my God, my strength, in whom I will trust; my buckler, and the horn of my salvation, and my high tower. I will call upon the Lord, who is worthy to be praised: so shall I be saved from mine enemies (Psalm 18:1-3).**

If there are children in the home, it is especially important to avoid reacting without prayerful thought. Your children need to be both your and your husband's number one consideration. No matter what their age, they do not deserve to be frightened and confused by the volatile energy that will accompany even the most toned down confrontation of these painful issues between their parents. If your children are young enough to still live under your roof, they are *not* old enough to psychologically or emotionally handle the painful issues you and your husband will need to be address and resolve.

Colleen: Be Willing to Listen to His Truth

As I enlarged my own understanding of prayer by studying the scriptures, especially the Book of Mormon, I began to realize that it was perfectly acceptable to Heavenly Father for me to turn my every thought into a prayer.[2] Thus, besides my morning and evening prayers, I began to deliberately turn to the Lord in my mind all through the day.

This was especially necessary in my relationship with my first husband. There was such a spirit of contention and bitterness emanating from him so much of the time, and I was so codependent (afraid of his anger and his efforts to blame and shame me for everything), I knew I was in no condition to trust my own feelings. I prayed pretty much continuously that the Lord would guide me and give me the ability to feel, think, and act as He would.

This same reliance on prayerful counsel with the Lord in my mind and in my heart became my anchor again as I began to interact with Phil about his addiction to pornography. Every time he admitted a slip to me, I turned immediately to the Savior in my mind, praying for the gift of *His* ability to hear my husband's truth with compassion—something that I couldn't even imagine doing on my own. As I allowed the Savior's love for Phil to come into my mind, I was able to recognize what a burden, scourge, and sorrow his addiction actually was to him. With the Savior's counsel and strength empowering me, I was able to reassure Phil that, just as his descent into addiction happened over a period of time, his deliverance from it would also take time.

I began to realize that it took a lot of pressure off him when he knew I wouldn't go into hysterics if he shared his reality with me. When Phil realized that he didn't have to let the slip isolate him, Satan lost yet one more lie that he had been using for so long to keep Phil in his control: The lie that I was too frail and unable to bear the truth, thus requiring him to protect me from the truth. *Protect* me from the *truth?* Just to read the words reveals the lie and the father of lies behind them.

Gradually, even though Phil's recovery path was littered with more slips and confessions, I came to genuinely value living in the light of truth. It helped me to remember that Satan thrives and revels in secrecy. The truth could and did make me free. It made me free to live in reality. It made me free to make my decisions from a more informed position. I had to embrace and accept the fact that progress is imperfect. The truth made us both become real to each other.

If you can both start telling the truth, including the less-than-happy, the less-than-admirable truth, you may also find yourself hearing the truth that you do both love each other, despite all your combined imperfections. You may find yourself becoming comrades in bearing one another's burdens with a compassion you've never known possible. This is when you can know that the pure love of Christ—of His Presence—has come to dwell in your marriage.

Phil: What It Was Like to Tell Colleen the Truth

I don't know that I have ever experienced a more uncomfortable situation than when I first had to admit my addiction to Colleen, unless it was during the next couple of years of recovery when I had to tell her of yet another slip. Doing so felt like the ultimate admission of failure, which was the one thing I never wanted to be in my wife's eyes. I know that the most important thing in my life should be what God thinks of me, but the truth is that it is tremendously important to me that my wife think well of me.

Another reason these experiences were so uncomfortable for me was that I had to listen to Colleen's reaction. It was excruciating to me to see how painful my slips were to her. Nevertheless, I needed to hear *her* truth. I needed to know that my actions were *not*, as Satan wanted me to believe, "only hurting myself."

The only reason I was able to reveal my slips to Colleen was that I knew from her past reactions that she would not turn away from me. She would not reject me because of my weakness. I knew there were limits to what she could tolerate, but it meant the world to me that she was willing to support me as long as I was trying to overcome my addiction.

Colleen: How to Respond to His Confessions

First of all, you need to seek the Lord's help to put your husband's slips into perspective, to see the reality of his behavior without projecting it into the future. Don't jump to the conclusion that a slip is a sign of full-scale relapse. Listen to his confession of temptation or a slip in judgment as calmly as possible. He needs you to hear him without making him "bad."

The chance that he is really a genuinely *bad* man who is beyond rescue is very small. Phil had to know that I did not define his addiction as a sign of an incurable flaw in his character. He also had to know that I didn't take his problem personally. It helped me to remember that if Phil was confessing a slip to me, he was doing what was probably the most humble thing he could do. He was repenting aloud and in front of the person who was most intimately involved in his recovery.

One way I knew that Phil's slips were slips and not relapses was because the Lord "whispered" the following insight into my mind: *The difference between a relapse and a slip is that a relapse is kept secret and thus goes on and on, feeding on its secrecy. A slip, by contrast, is not kept secret but is dealt with promptly by the addict going to someone who understands recovery and will listen to him as he tells the truth.*

Please pray about this insight and see if there is truth in it for you.

By telling you his truth—that he's still struggling—your husband is asking for your support in sharing the burden of another slip. In return, it is essential that he be willing to do the same for you, to listen to you share *your* truth. He has to be willing to hear your honest feelings, and you have an obligation to share them and not stuff them down and gloss over them. It doesn't allow the healing light or Spirit of Truth to come into your relationship if either of you think you have to keep truth back from each other.

Admittedly, it is a pretty challenging thing to think that the process of recovery may go on for some time and that you both will have to share the burden of how much it hurts. But if you do not share the burden, the healing won't be shared either. Only if you both communicate openly can the Spirit of the Lord enter into your hearts and minds and bring you both into oneness with the Savior.

Sharing Your Truth without Tearing Him Down

As we testified earlier, this sharing of the heartache and burden addiction has created in both your lives will take super-human strength. Both of you will need the strength only the Lord can give you to last through the angry stage, so that you can finally feel the deeper truth— just how *sad* you feel and how many tears you need to cry.

Your first impulse may be to judge your husband and call him names, but those are actions prompted by the adversary to drive a wedge of hatefulness between you and him and to further demoralize both of you. Judging is not the same as expressing your feelings. It may be difficult to separate the two, but if you ask Him, the Lord will guide you to recognize the difference and express your true feelings without judging your husband as evil.

Understand, though, we're not saying that you should lie or pretend confidence in your husband that you don't have. We just know by our own experience as a husband and wife living through these painful moments: *If you will turn to the Lord, you will find confidence in Him—in Christ—and the ability to respond with HIS grace toward your husband.*

Just as you sought the inspiration, grace, and power of the Lord to know how to *listen* to hard things, it is important that you seek inspiration and power from Him to know how to *say* the hard things you need to say. After you have sought the Lord's love and truth for your husband, you will be better prepared to be the Lord's instrument in communicating with him.

Colleen: Be Very Prayerful About Wanting to Know Details

One of the hardest things for many wives to let go of is the compulsion to know the details of their husbands' episodes of acting out. In my case, I have to admit that I didn't struggle much with this. I'm not sure exactly why. I think part of it might have come from the fact that I had spent several years studying Twelve Step recovery for my own addiction. I knew that the details of an addict's acting out were beside the point.

I came to realize in the course of my recovery that the phrase in Step Five that recommends confession of "the *exact nature* of my wrongs," was not referring to my acting out. It was referring to the exact nature of my *wrong thinking* that set me up to act out. I didn't need to tell my spouse or even my sponsor the details of what I had consumed during an episode of my compulsive eating. The motives and thinking that led up to it were what I really needed to face and admit to another person.

Thus because of my own background in recovery, I was able to understand and accept the counsel of our prophets and of professional counselors. They all testify that dwelling on the details of a transgression isn't helpful for anyone involved. The wisdom of this advice has been confirmed by the testimonies of other women whose marriages have survived the crisis of their husbands' sexual addictions.

I have come to believe that when the Lord, through the scriptures and the modern prophets, tells us we should "remember the sin no more," it is *the details* of our sins, as well as those of others, He is asking us to forget. Obviously, the Lord would not ask us to totally forget that these challenging experiences ever happened, because that would negate what we have learned and would set us up to make the same mistakes all over again. I believe that what He wants us to do is to stop obsessing about the particulars.

Both of you will be plagued by rehearsing the details. It isn't necessary. It only inflames the situation and spreads the infection of sin from one mind to another. Consequently, it is much wiser to allow your husband to simply admit that he's had another slip and let it go at that.

Colleen: Letting Others Know the Truth

Even after all the painful sharing between you and your husband, there is still one more way that you must allow the light of truth to penetrate your life in order to fully heal from the effects of your loved one's addiction. You must be willing to talk to other people about it. You must be willing to admit that you can't do this alone, that you need support.

Satan will try with every form of persuasive thought to convince you not to let anyone else know, but do not believe this false idea. Your husband may very likely be one of the voices begging, persuading, *demanding* that you not tell anyone else. You would be unwise to listen. To agree to keep sin a secret and thus avoid confessing to a priesthood authority is, in a small, personal way, the equivalent of entering into a "secret combination." By keeping this secret, you are in effect keeping acts of darkness from being brought into the light.

In my first marriage, when I became aware of my husband's sexual acting out, I came to a place where I could not keep up the family façade that everything was "just fine." (The irony is that I found out later that many of my closest friends could see the cracks in the façade already and knew better than I did that things weren't going well.) I came to a place where the **"whited sepulchres"**[3] of what everyone else thought of me and my family, could not be maintained any more. I came to a place where I cried out, "Give me honesty or give me death!"

In my experience, no spiritual health or growth can go on in the presence of lies. Appearances might be kept up, but on the inside, in private, the presence of secret sin will poison the whole family unit. I had to go to someone and tell the truth. I couldn't pretend anymore. I couldn't bear the burden alone, enabling the lies to go on.

Talking to the Bishop

One of the first people we would counsel you to prayerfully consider turning to is your bishop, branch president or stake president. Once again, Satan will try to bring up a hundred reasons why you shouldn't do this but you must not believe his lying thoughts. The reality is that bishops and stake presidents are receiving more and more training and counseling from the General Authorities pertaining specifically to this issue of sexual addiction and all the forms of sin it can take. Don't be afraid to talk to your local priesthood leaders.

I hope that when you talk with the bishop that you can talk plainly and honestly. Lay it all out, all of the emotions. Sometimes I feel when I meet with a bishop that I need to put on my Sunday face. I have decided that doesn't do any of us any good, because we are not able to clearly express the struggles or desires of our hearts when we are pretending to be a good little soldier.
— *Rosalyn*

Your husband may accuse you of betraying him for going to the bishop about his problem and not leaving that for him to do. Do not believe this way of thinking. The truth is you are not going to the bishop about your husband's problem. You are going about yours.

You need to separate your husband's challenge (the fact that he's developed a sexual addiction) from your problem (you're living with someone with a sexual addiction). You need to realize that your bishop is just that—*your* bishop. You can go to him for your own sake, not in an attempt to fix your husband. Go to your bishop in the same spirit you approach the Lord—seeking counsel and guidance, strength and blessings *for yourself*. It's not tattling on your husband to go to your bishop for counsel pertaining to *your* challenges.

You know the LDS Young Women theme? "We will stand as witnesses of God, at all times, in all things, and in all places." Stand up for what is right, and by so doing, you won't enable him anymore. My suggestion: go to the bishop to support YOU.   — *Nancy*

Phil: Living in the Light of Truth Brings You to Know the Lord

After all the cautionary messages in this chapter about noticing negative behavior, we would like to conclude on a positive note by inviting you to have faith in the Savior to work a mighty change in your husband's heart as recovery progresses. True recovery is identical with the process of true repentance and redemption. True recovery includes becoming converted to the Savior Himself, which conversion is far more than just being a member of His Church. As Elder Richard G. Scott of the Quorum of the Twelve Apostles testified, being active in the Church and even being able to express a testimony of the Church is possible without having experienced what it means to come unto Christ and become converted to Him personally.[4]

Some years ago, I wrote a booklet entitled *Dear Bishop*. Though it was addressed to bishops, I wrote it with the hope that my experience as a recovering addict and my work one-on-one with many of my brethren might be of value to anyone trying to discern whether someone they care about is really recovering from addiction. It is so important to never forget that recovery is far more than a certain length of abstinence. The following list includes some signs that I suggest a bishop (or anyone else) might look for as an indication that a man is on the road to a genuine "mighty change of heart" and not just a temporary change of habit. I have adapted the wording to apply to your life with your husband.

- Your husband will be more humble and more willing to talk about his weaknesses and past mistakes. This is because shame will diminish as the Savior lifts his burden.

- Your husband will be more willing to talk about his daily struggles. Instead of brushing off questions with glib reassurances, such as "I'm fine," "It's great," or "Nothing to worry about," he will be willing to share the reality that he deals with temptations and has a continuing need for the Lord.

- He will tell you if he slips. The difference between a slip and a relapse is whether or not it is kept secret. If your husband is willing to quickly admit a moment of weakness and put it behind him, it is most likely only a slip. The Lord has said, **"By this ye may know if a man repenteth of his sins...he will confess them and forsake them."**[5] There may be several rounds of confession before the final forsaking happens. This is to be expected when overcoming any bad habit or addiction.

- He will take responsibility for his own actions and sins and will not be prone to blame others—not you, nor his parents, his leaders, or his past.

- He will exhibit a spirit of peace and calm. The Savior promised that He would give us peace if we come unto Him. This peace should be observable in someone that is coming to Him as often as they need to in order to overcome addiction.

- He will have a deeper relationship with the Savior. When you ask him to talk about the Savior, his replies will frequently come with emotion and will indicate a personal relationship, not just "Sunday School" answers. He will show evidence of coming to know the Savior as a person, not just as an image or a concept.

- He will have a desire to help others recover. He will be grateful for a chance to share what he has learned and experienced with others who still struggle (when the Spirit directs).

- Because of the gratitude to the Lord a recovering addict feels for this miraculous change, your husband will have a desire to serve Him, not only in public callings, but also in private acts of service.

- Since this miracle has only been brought about through a close relationship with the Lord, your husband will understand the need to stay close to the Lord through a continuing program of regular spiritual activities and will continue to pray, to ponder, and to capture personal insights from the scriptures.

- Your husband's improved relationship with the Lord will be evident in his prayers, which will be heartfelt and meaningful. Invite him to pray with you so that you have the opportunity to feel the spirit of his prayers.

Of course, people vary. Not everyone responds in the same way, but these are some general guidelines of what recovery from addiction looks like. We hope that these ideas may help you hold on to your faith and trust that the process of recovery is working to bring him, and you as well, to know the Lord one-on-one, as your Savior and dearest Friend.

1. Doctrine & Covenants 93:29.

2. Doctrine & Covenants 6:36; Alma 37:37; 3 Nephi 20:1.

3. Matthew 23:27.

4. Richard G. Scott, "Full Conversion Brings Happiness," *Ensign*, May 2002.

5. Doctrine & Covenants 58:43.

11 *Setting Boundaries Isn't About Controlling Him*

Setting boundaries is usually thought of as putting limits or restrictions on what someone else does or doesn't do. Setting boundaries as part of your recovery is the exact opposite idea. This chapter is about you taking your attention—all of it—off of your loved one's choices and putting it on the one person's choices you can actually change—your own. Setting boundaries isn't about controlling *him*; it is about honoring *you*. It's about honoring your agency and changing the way you choose to participate in your relationship with your husband.

It Doesn't Work to "Parent" an Adult

Most of us are familiar with the idea of setting boundaries with children. We often say things like, "If you leave the yard without getting your chores done, then…" and we apply a consequence. By doing this we are trying to shape behavior, teach values, and promote our child's character development.

In setting a boundary in a marriage, however, we are not trying to shape the other person's behavior. Your spouse is not a child. He is an adult. By the time a person has reached adulthood, the shaping of his (or her) behavior and character must be entirely their own responsibility. To parent another adult is the equivalent of exercising **"unrighteous dominion."**[1] His choice of behavior is sovereign and can only be modified according to his own will.

While you do have the right to express your feelings, trying to control your husband's behavior can often have the effect of encouraging his inclination to defend his own agency. Paradoxically, this gives the adversary, Satan, an opening to tempt him with the lie that acting out is his "right," his way of demonstrating that he will not be forced. Thus the father of lies twists a truth to serve his purposes.

Colleen: Seeking the Lord's Counsel in Setting Boundaries

Agency is the freedom to direct our own lives. As daughters of God we have exactly the same right as our husbands to seek direct and personal revelation for our own sake. We must turn to the Lord to work out our own salvation, take charge of our own lives, get honest with ourselves and with others about our boundaries, and determine if and when we need to adjust them.

One of the realities each of us as wives must face at this point is the truth that our husbands do not hold ultimate authority over us, even when they are being worthy. The Family Proclamation gives this beautiful explanation of the relationship between a husband and a wife:

> In these sacred responsibilities, fathers and mothers are obligated to help one another as *equal* partners" ("The Family: A Proclamation to the World," *Ensign*, Nov. 1995, 102; emphasis added).

President Spencer W. Kimball gave us great counsel on the partnership of a marriage, saying:

> When we speak of marriage as a partnership, let us speak of marriage as a *full* partnership. We do not want our LDS women to be *silent* partners or *limited* partners in that eternal assignment! Please be a *contributing* and *full* partner (Edward L. Kimball, ed. *The Teachings of Spencer W. Kimball*, 315, emphasis added).

President Kimball also declared, "We have heard of men who have said to their wives, 'I hold the priesthood and you've got to do what I say.'" President Kimball went on to decisively reject abuse of priesthood authority in a marriage, declaring that such a man "should not be honored in his priesthood" (*Ibid.*, 316).

What I have done this week that has been so good for me is to focus on my relationship with God, building my faith in myself, and letting my husband deal with his challenges. I set prayerfully determined boundaries. And you know what? I have felt more peace than I have in a while. My husband sees that I am serious and he is making a new effort to get in touch with himself and God and get to where he needs to be. It is terrifying but peaceful. My hope and prayer is that he finds God. That is the ultimate desire of my heart.   — Amy

---

What Are Reasonable Boundaries?

Once a woman accepts the fact that she is fully capable and equally privileged to seek and receive direct, personal guidance from the Lord pertaining to her own best interests and her children's as well, it becomes time to consider some of the boundaries she may need or want to establish.

As we offer these thoughts, we must remind you once again that, as with all the counsel in these chapters, these are only suggestions. They are based on a combination of our own experience and the experiences of the many sisters with whom we have had the opportunity to converse. We are sure that as you associate with others in recovery, you will be exposed to other ideas pertaining to setting boundaries. Remember, boundaries are the limits that you need to put in place in order to be honest about what you can endure. They do not define a punishment when others choose not to adhere to them.

Putting internet filters on your home computer. It goes without saying that if you have children, you are right to be concerned that they might be exposed to internet pornography and become addicted themselves. At the very least, you may fear that their discovery of their father's secret indulgences will destroy their respect for him. Keeping children safe from inadvertent exposure to pornography on the internet is the main reason we wholeheartedly support the use of filters and passwords on your home computer, as well as keeping your computer(s) in public areas of the home.

Whether an internet filter will help your husband or not depends very much on his motivation. Some men report that a filter only provides an extra challenge rather than an actual deterrent. (For a more complete discussion of filters and other "prevention" methods, go to www.windhavenpublishing.com for a free download of Phil's booklet, *Dear Bishop*).

Limiting other media that may be brought into your home. It is true that we can't prevent our children (and grandchildren) from being exposed to pornographic images when they go out into the world. It is everywhere and extremely accessible. But the home should be a safe haven—a place where the world does not intrude. You have every right to insist that your husband not bring any sexually explicit or suggestive materials into your home. You do not need to tolerate it under any circumstances, even if your husband should argue for his "rights." Suggestive magazines, movies, and other media have no place in your home.

What about cable or satellite television? Each of us must decide this issue for our own family, but we believe it is essential to become "a peculiar people" in this respect, especially considering how commonly amoral behaviors are being portrayed as normal in the world at large. Missing out on some otherwise desirable programming may be a worthwhile price to pay for protecting your children and yourself from the filth that typically comes with most cable and satellite packages. At the very least, consider a service that provides parental lockdowns and passcodes to block objectionable material.

While it is inevitable that your children will be exposed to material in other places—at friends' homes, at movies, or at school—that you would not allow in your own home, setting this boundary communicates your values to your children. It is very important that you as a parent define sexuality for your children as a divine attribute and a sacred and joyful experience when shared in the sanctity of marriage.

What about the good reasons for having the internet and cable TV? What do you do if TV or the internet is a problem in your home? What if you can't get your husband to disconnect them? Do you act on your own and do it anyway? What if the internet is an important part of someone's employment or education? What about using it for doing family history research?

It's very true that there is a lot of good available through these modern forms of communication, as well as bad. These are decisions we can't make for you. Each family's situation is different, and one size or solution does not fit all. In all these decisions, our final counsel can only be to urge you to seek the Lord and His counsel. What arrangement with these forms of media do you feel truly peaceful about? The Lord will whisper peace to your mind concerning this (and all things). He knows your husband, your children and you. He knows your needs, and what it will take for addiction to be conquered in your home. Keep your heart and mind open to His directions. They might have to involve some pretty strict boundaries—at least for a time.

What affects your own intimate relations as a couple. It is a sad fact that some men who have become addicted to pornography and other forms of unrighteous sexual behavior will try to involve their wives in their acting out. A wife who notices marked or unwelcome changes in her husband's sexual behavior or desires will generally feel uncomfortable. If this is happening in your marriage, we hope you will believe that it is your God-given right to say, "Wait a minute."

The fact is, a husband and wife's sexual experience with each other is one of the most spiritually symbolic and emotionally significant pillars of their relationship. It is an area that must convey the deepest respect and mutually satisfying communion between the two of you. Although it is often awkward to talk about these sensitive matters, such a discussion may be essential to establishing a relationship that is fulfilling to and respectful of both partners.

President David O. McKay said this about the marriage relationship:

> **Let us instruct...young men throughout the Church, to know that a woman should be queen of her own body. The marriage covenant does not give the man the right to enslave her, or to abuse her, or to use her merely for the gratification of his passion. Your marriage ceremony does not give you that right (President David O. McKay, *Conference Report*, April 1952, General Priesthood Meeting).**

For you to set boundaries regarding what you feel comfortable about in your marriage relationship is a vital step in preserving your own dignity and self-respect. In all likelihood, you will also find your husband respecting you more as you respect yourself.

Some wives may feel that their husband's behavior is so contaminated by his indulgences in pornography that they cannot continue sexual relations until things change. This is a very personal decision and one you need to consider very prayerfully. Still, do not doubt your own true feelings. You are not in the wrong to have your sexual experiences be the expression of not only a sacred, but also a satisfying, enjoyable experience for both of you. Every woman who has given her life and her procreative powers to her husband deserves to be cherished, and not used as a sex object. President McKay in his conference talk to the men in the priesthood session continued to speak plainly of the standard of behavior the Lord expects of husbands toward their wives:

> **Second, let [husbands] remember that gentleness and consideration after the ceremony is just as appropriate and necessary and beautiful as gentleness and consideration before the wedding.**

Third, let us realize that manhood is not undermined by the practicing of continence, notwithstanding what some psychiatrists claim. Chastity is the crown of beautiful womanhood, and self-control is the source of true manhood (*Ibid.*).

Many sexually addicted men go into marriage thinking that getting married will solve their sexual addiction—kind of like a drug addict thinking that switching to a prescription makes his addiction legal. You, as a wife, do not need to feel like you are being selfish or that you are causing him to act out, if you need to be honest about your intimate relations with him. The truth is, marriage does not give a man a *carte blanche* sexual arrangement with his spouse. A husband who is willing to live in recovery from sexual addiction must be constantly on his guard against the temptation to think of sex as a means of getting his own personal needs met. To think of sex with his wife in that way is merely a continuation of the selfishness that is the hallmark of addiction.

Extramarital involvement. Addiction is a progressive disease and it is not uncommon that what starts out as a fantasy relationship with images and movies advances to interactions with real women (or men) in strip clubs, massage parlors, or extramarital affairs. If your husband's addiction has taken him this far, our hearts go out to you. Admittedly, this is like finding out that a cancer has gone from stage one to stage four. This is clearly an area where you will want to honor yourself with some serious boundaries, beginning with protecting yourself from possible sexually transmitted diseases.

Other "side effects" of the addiction. Another unfortunate reality a wife must face is that her husband's sexual addiction can affect other aspects of his character. For example, the addict frequently resorts to lies to keep from being found out. In some cases addiction drives a person to steal to be able to pursue the activity. Being vague and forgetful about where money is spent is also common. Often the lying and deceit are the most painful part of the experience for the wife. You have a right to talk with your husband about these behaviors.

Addiction can undermine the addict's character in ways other than honesty. Depending on his personality, your husband's behavior toward you and the children may begin to slide into thoughtlessness or into actual emotional, physical or sexual abuse. Abuse in any form must not be ignored or excused. Whatever your husband's problems, you have a right to personal dignity and even more importantly, to personal safety.

If you are experiencing abuse of any kind in your home, you need to stand up for yourself calmly but firmly, knowing that in the eyes of the Lord, you are 100% in the right. You do not have to resort to rage and retaliation in any form. In fact those ways of responding will only be counterproductive, fueling your husband's excuses for acting out. Let your response to his unkindness and mean-spiritedness be as calm and dignified as possible, seeking for yourself the Lord's strength and dignity. The Lord did not give you and your children to your husband to be the victims of Satan's hold on him. If your husband refuses to respect these basic rights, something deeper is wrong, and we urge you to counsel with your bishop or with a professional who deals with marriage and/or women's issues. Most importantly, give the highest priority to making sure you and your children are safe.

Phil: How Knowing Colleen's Boundaries Has Blessed My Life

I met Colleen when my first wife Kathy and I started attending Twelve Step (Heart-t-Heart) meetings in her home. After Kathy passed away and Colleen and I became engaged, I was in a recovery program and was gaining better abstinence, although I did have a few slips in the first year we were married. As I contemplated marriage to Colleen, I knew I needed to make some changes.

I had accumulated some R-rated videos and some PG-13 rated ones that had nudity in them. I knew Colleen had a definite boundary of not watching R-rated movies and I did not want to have any around when we got married. It was a difficult decision for me to get rid of some of these movies. After all (argued the natural man in me) I paid a lot of money for these, and some of them contained genuinely excellent acting. And besides the nudity was usually brief... On and on went the rationalizations until I finally asked the Lord for the grace to let them go, which I was then able to do. He also helped me to dismiss any thought of reselling them or giving them away. Instead, He counseled me to destroy them. In time I also became willing to let the objectionable PG-13 movies go as well.

After some discussion, Colleen and I agreed that we would forego the expense and temptation of having cable or satellite television in our home. That may sound pretty extreme, but it was a sacrifice we were both willing to make for the sake of keeping several potential addictions out of our home. We both agreed that besides the constant likelihood of exposure to sexually enticing material via the multitude of channels, there was also the temptation to spend too many of our own precious hours watching others portray pretend lives. We've learned to "subsist" (by modern standards) on the several educational broadcast channels we enjoy and the DVDs we rent. It may sound pretty spartan to some, but I am grateful that we made these decisions. I am certain they have helped me maintain my abstinence, especially during the beginning years when my recovery was most vulnerable.

When Your Honest Boundaries Seem to Have No Effect on Him

Before you take your husband's continued acting out as a personal offense, you must remember that it is very nearly impossible for most men—even genuinely good men—to stop acting out immediately. Sometimes it can take quite a while after they have started studying and applying recovery principles to see a substantial change in behaviors and attitudes.

Never forget your husband is *addicted*. That means that in the beginning of his efforts to recover, no matter how much your husband may want to change, or how much he may truly love you and your children, he must humble himself and seek a *spiritual* answer. Nothing anyone else says or does—even a beloved wife setting her boundaries—can bring about the "mighty change of heart" that must be the foundation of a successful recovery effort for him. You must also never forget that Satan is the ultimate enemy, prompting you to be impatient and obsessed with your husband's progress.

If, on the other hand, you honestly and truly—with meekness and with much humbling of yourself in prayerful soul-searching—find yourself at the absolute limit of how long you can wait for his recovery, then it may well be that the Lord is giving you what is often referred to as "divine discontent." It may be that the Lord is prompting you to be an instrument in His hands to help your husband "hit bottom" and seek recovery more seriously than he has so far.

This is really where the rubber hits the road, as the old saying goes. This is where you (and your husband) find out if you really mean what you say. If boundaries are to have any validity at all, you must be prepared to follow through with whatever response you honestly feel is necessary. Your response could range from needing to abstain from sexual intimacy with him to asking him to move out of the bedroom or even out of the house.

Remember, when dealing with an adult, you can't set boundaries in an attempt to control the other person. You can only set boundaries that define what matters most to you and what you feel the Lord has counseled you to endure or not to endure. Keep inventorying your own motives and be sure you are not doing anything in an attempt to punish or change him.

---

1. Doctrine & Covenants 121:39.

12 Calling a Time Out

Calling a time out in a ball game is not a bad thing. In fact, it is a very good thing. Putting a child in time out, as most parents know, is usually not a bad thing, either. It's a good thing. It gives everyone a chance to disengage and calm down, cool off. Taking a time out may be a good thing in a marriage, too. If you have tried and tried to work things out with your husband, and if the Spirit is confirming to you that you have tried long enough, then perhaps it's time to consider taking a time out. A time out is an opportunity to reset one's thinking—to reassess where one is in relationship to various aspects of one's life.

Church discipline, such as probation, being disfellowshipped or excommunicated, could be considered a form of time out that local church leaders may implement in a spirit of love in order to emphasize the seriousness of someone's situation. Similarly, there are various kinds of time outs that may need to be prayerfully implemented in order to facilitate recovery in a marriage damaged by sexual addiction.

A Time Out Is a Serious Decision

Making the decision to have a time out requires you to be patient and very prayerful in finding an inspired balance between mercy and justice. Only the Lord Himself can bless you to know the right combination of patience for your husband and courage to admit you cannot *honestly* continue with the *status quo*. This is a great balancing act. On the one side, your husband may be about to change, and your support may help him. On the other hand, there are an unfortunate number of men who postpone seeking genuine recovery until the reality of what they are risking is brought home to them through serious consequences. If you come to this point, your husband must then decide how he will respond, whether he will increase his dedication to recovery or continue in the direction he is currently choosing to go.

Because calling any kind of a time out is such a serious decision, we encourage you to counsel with your bishop, with a professional marriage counselor, with parents or other family members, or with a combination of such supportive people. No matter who else you counsel with, you need to pray continually for the ultimate guidance, which will be whispered to your heart and mind by your Father in Heaven. When you know beyond all explanation and all defense that the decision is confirmed to you by a feeling of peace—even if it is a *painful* peace—then you may know you are acting in harmony with God, just as the following scripture testifies:

> **I will tell you in your mind and in your heart, by the Holy Ghost, which shall come upon you and which shall dwell in your heart. Now, behold, this is the spirit of revelation (Doctrine & Covenants 8:2-3).**

One reason for calling a time out may be that you need some time and space to counsel with others and with the Lord about one or more of the following realities:

- The Spirit of the Lord witnesses to you to separate temporarily in order to seriously consider what is at stake if either one or both partners do not embrace the principles of recovery and allow the power of the Savior's atonement to change their hearts.

- As painful as it may be, sometimes it is actually given of the Spirit of the Lord for a marriage to end. You may be feeling the growing witness of this reality. We will address this possibility further in Chapter 13, "What If We Can't Reconcile."

- You may have become aware that your husband's addiction has led him to break the laws of the land as well as the law of the Lord. We will address this devastating situation in "What If a Criminal Act Has Been Committed?" in the Appendix.

Calling a Time Out from Sexual Relations

When a marriage has been damaged to a serious degree, continuing to have a sexual relationship may give the message that everything is all right when the truth is that the marriage is in serious trouble. The sexual relationship between a husband and wife is intended to express love and commitment. When those elements are missing, as evidenced in the most severe kinds of sexual addiction, sex between the partners loses its meaning, and becomes a lie.

Whether this time out is temporary or becomes permanent depends on what your husband decides to do in terms of recovery and repentance. We hope that a time out is effective in helping your husband reassess his commitment to you and your marriage.

_____

After my husband's slip, I prayerfully decided that I needed to have a period of abstinence in our marriage. I spoke with my sponsor and read the Abstinence section from Working the S-Anon Program. We sat down and had a long discussion about my desire to have a period of abstinence in our marriage.

At first, my husband was very upset. He said he didn't know how to be roommates with his wife. When I explained to him that I just wanted to take sex off the table and that I wanted us to focus on our relationship, he started to listen. We needed to court again. I needed to feel safe and he needed to get sober. Once he opened the door to the addiction, it took him time to regain his sobriety and get the thoughts out of his mind. We needed to rediscover why we love each other and feel close to each other without sex.

I told him that we could still hold hands, hug, kiss and hold each other. We set a date for when we would reevaluate how we both felt and then decide if we would be intimate again. This experience has been very helpful for us. I have set my boundaries and we are rediscovering our relationship. We are dating again and healing.   — Jessica

Calling a Time Out from Living Together

Physical closeness between marriage partners almost always reflects how close they feel emotionally. The truth is, where there is no hand-holding, no eye-to-eye contact, no small, *non-sexual* touches exchanged between a husband and wife, having sex can become an act of dishonesty. In order to restore a sense of integrity in such a situation, there may need to be a period of physical separation. This may first be expressed when the wife asks her husband to move out of the bedroom and sleep somewhere else in the house. If this level of time out does not bring an increase in humility and willingness to communicate, it may be necessary to go to the next level and ask him to move out of the house.

Perhaps time apart will help a husband who is wandering (mentally, emotionally, or physically) to appreciate what he will lose if his behavior does not change. It may also be a time for the wife to do some clear thinking without interruption. Based on this time of reflection, she may realize how good her marriage really is. On the other hand, she may see how bad it really is.

Be certain that your motivation for asking for these periods of time out is for the sake of trying to ultimately bring healing. If you are certain this is your heart's intent, then you can know that whatever the results, your motives were right. Then, if he chooses to harden his heart toward you even more, you will know that your decision to call a time out was not the reason your marriage ended—if that is what comes to pass.

I wonder if I were to separate from him for a season and allow him to focus on himself and where he would be without us, that maybe then he would desire to take the necessary steps. The other side of me says he needs me to get through this, and he needs the kids. They need him. I fear being alone, and yet I already am in so many ways. I want to have things work out for everyone's sake, but I also know that I cannot work everything out on my own. There's my part, the Lord's part and the scary part, that's my husband's part.   — Denise

---

Phil: Staying Isn't Necessarily Helping the Children

While it is true that impatience and even some degree of rudeness and anger is usually one of the symptoms of a person secretly acting out in their sexual addiction, it is very important for you to be prayerfully aware of how such an atmosphere is affecting your children. They do not deserve the kind of emotional and mental confusion and uncertainty that living with a practicing addict brings. That spinning out of control in the "cycle of addiction" that we discussed in Chapter Four, where the addict is loving one day and irrationally irritated the next, can seriously damage a child's sense of security and self-esteem. Children, almost without exception, jump to the conclusion (even more than you do) that whatever the problem is, it's about them.

I do not believe it is the will of our Father in Heaven that any woman or child be subjected to *chronic* rudeness, blame, and shame from the husband or father-figure in their lives. This is especially true when those men have made covenants to represent the Lord's priesthood. Everyone is human, of course, and everyone gets grouchy sometimes. That's not the dynamic I'm talking about. Abuse is the deepening of darkness that comes into the spiritual atmosphere of a home when a man begins to do as is described in this verse:

> **When we undertake to *cover our sins,* or to gratify our pride, our vain ambition, or to *exercise control or dominion or compulsion* upon the souls of the children of men, in any degree of unrighteousness, behold, the heavens withdraw themselves; the Spirit of the Lord is grieved (Doctrine & Covenants 121:37; emphasis added).**

Alcoholics Anonymous (the AA Big Book) describes this as men who are "thoroughly bad-intentioned" and to whom "no amount of patience will ever make any difference."[1] Staying with a man who refuses to seek recovery and instead allows his repressed shame and guilt to take the form of maliciousness and abuse toward you and your children is doing that man no good, and in fact, is doing your children great harm. Even if there is little physical abuse, the emotional, verbal, and spiritual abuse can be even more damaging to them. Daughters learn that they deserve this treatment and sons learn that males have the right to take their unhappiness out on others.

In addition to the emotional damage such a habitually angry person can do to his children, there is a deeper, spiritual damage that occurs. It is commonly felt that a child's first and maybe longest lasting picture of their Heavenly Father is based on their parents, especially their father. If the father in the home is chronically and irrationally angry, the child concludes that God, too, is impatient and inconsistent; he learns to fear God and to avoid coming to Him. Of the men I have done Twelve Step work with, the ones who have the hardest time forming a relationship with Heavenly Father and Jesus are the ones who had angry fathers.

Colleen: Indications That It Might Be Best for Him to Leave

If you are contemplating whether or not you need to ask your husband for a temporary separation, I would like to offer the following thoughts for your prayerful consideration. These were realities that I was living with in my first marriage and that I have heard described by scores of other women who are dealing with sexually addicted husbands.

There is a definite lightening of the atmosphere in your home when he's away for a few days. One of the things I had to eventually admit was the difference in the feeling in my home when my first husband was there compared with times when he would go away on scouting or business trips. It was like all the little prey animals would come out of the shadows where they usually hid from the predator. We would all relax and laugh and play. It was as if the sunshine had come out from behind the clouds. When he was home there was always a feeling of "cloudiness." Sometimes the "clouds" were high and hazy and a bit of light would filter through, but most days they were glowering and dark. The children and I lived in a "hunkered down" state of emotion. We were never sure who would be the next target of his sarcasm or scorn.

His attempts to make physical contact with you always have a sexual overtone. As we mentioned earlier, where there is no touching, kissing, or holding for purely affectionate reasons, all intimacy comes with sexual overtones. When this is the case, then something very foundational is missing in your husband's need for you.

Love does not begin with sex. If physical interactions with your husband are primarily sexual in intent, such interactions most likely do *not* represent love. My first husband had no time for me. Other things like scouting, working, church responsibilities, or television were always more important—until we were in bed. Then he was finally willing to pay attention to me, to touch me. Even then there were very few kisses, mostly just touching, immediate arousal, use of my body for sexual release, and then an immediate return to ignoring me. No shared emotional afterglow or cuddling.

When I met Kathy and Phil, one of the first things I noticed about them was how close they liked to be in a way that was publicly appropriate. They sat close to each other. They stood close to each other. They leaned on each other, putting their arms around each other. They smiled at each other and laughed in unison a lot. There was a genuine *friendliness* between them. I remember being around them at meetings and later pondering how they modeled the only kind of relationship I would settle for if I were to ever become seriously involved with someone again.

Today, with things having turned out the way they have, I think very fondly of Kathy and how she "trained Phil right." When I say that, though, I'm just kidding. I know that the willingness to be that kind of husband in that kind of friendly, affectionate relationship with a woman arises from Phil's own heart. Eleven years of living with him has taught me that struggling with an addiction does *not* have to make a man (or woman) unaffectionate physically or unfriendly emotionally.

He knows there are recovery resources but he avoids them. Phil and I are shocked at how many cases we have become aware of over the years where the husband actually knows there's help for his sexual addiction but refuses to take advantage of it. He thinks they're stupid, or he doesn't believe they will help, or he thinks he's not doing anything *that* wrong.

It's one thing for a man to be going to meetings, working with a sponsor, actively reading literature and most especially praying and seeking communion/oneness with the Lord and still having slips. It's another situation, entirely, to have a husband who knows there's help out there and refuses to participate in it. Or maybe he's been to a few meetings and learned enough recovery jargon to "talk the talk," as they say, but he isn't "walking the walk." That's the way my first husband was. He attended some recovery meetings but was bored and uncomfortable with what went on there. He thought it was a waste of time, a place for wimps and liars, for people just pretending to want to be better. He didn't need to hang out with "those kind of people."

The occasional positive moment is being swallowed up by the negative moments. I lived in denial about how bad things were for so long, partly because I was willing to subsist on a starvation ration of positive, happy moments in our home. Remember that every man can behave in a good, kind, flattering way some of the time. Be honest with yourself about just how frequently the hard times are happening and how long they are lasting. Be honest about how demoralized you and your children are becoming. Above all else, seek to comprehend the Lord's love for you and your children. Pray for the Holy Spirit to convey that love to you in a real and tangible way, so that you can begin to have a gauge in your heart of what love feels like.

Many wives living with predominantly dark and abusive marriages do so because it's what we've seen our mothers live with. We hang on because we think this is as good as we can hope for. It took me twenty-three years to finally allow the love of God to come into my heart and give me a testimony that what I was living with was not in harmony with His love for me. I pray that you will know you can seek His guidance and feel His direct love for you. Nothing will do more to light your way through the decisions you must make and the challenges you face.

The Spirit of Truth testifies to you that separating is the only thing left to do. I'm not sure if anyone other than another believing, active LDS woman who has faced this option (asking your husband to leave your bed and eventually to leave the home) can begin to imagine what it feels like to surrender to this truth. Everything in me cried out, "No! No! This can't be the answer!" That is, everything cried out except the deep, unavoidable stillness that came over me when I sought the Lord.

Even in the temple, even after much fasting and prayer, even after much counseling with every good person I knew, I could not shake the witness I felt. I knew for months—maybe as much as a year or more—that I was coming to the end of my ability to pretend that having sexual relations with my first husband was an honest act on my part. I knew I was only going through the motions, and I'm sure he knew it too. He didn't seem to care. Going through the motions seemed to be fine with him. He didn't seem to want or need any other kind of relationship with me except the physical kind. In other words, sex, housekeeping, sex, child-care, sex, meals...

If you've been in the kind of situation I'm describing, you'll know what I mean. If you haven't, you'll think I'm exaggerating. Those of us who have lived with this degree of deterioration of the marriage and this degree of degradation of one's self as a worthwhile human being for ten, fifteen, or twenty years, can't help it if others think we're exaggerating— or worse yet, that we're lying. I knew when I was lying. It was when I tried to keep up the façade that everything was good enough, that everything was working. I knew when I was finally being honest. It was when I admitted that it wasn't working, and I asked for separate sleeping arrangements, and finally for separate living arrangements.

Trust the Lord, even if His counsel seems counterintuitive, even when it feels like you can't make it another day. If you feel His witness to go on just one more day, do so. Or if despite all your reasons not to separate, you feel Him testifying to you that you must, then do so. He will be with you as you humbly try to discern and live the truth as sincerely as you can.

Colleen: The Right Time to Say "It's Enough"

After you have prayerfully evaluated the issues listed above, there may still be some doubts remaining. How do you know *you* are ready to take this step? Maybe all the signs indicate that he needs a separation to happen and you have to admit that things aren't getting any better as they are, but what about your feelings? What about your motives? How do you know you have really had "enough?" I would suggest that it is the right time when you are ready to go on with *your* life, no matter what his response to your truth may be. In other words, when you can say, "It's enough," and *mean* it.

If you haven't reached this point of truly feeling that you have had enough and that you really can go on by yourself if you have to, no matter how he decides to respond, then perhaps confronting this subject isn't the right decision yet. A half-hearted decision is no good. If you don't really mean it yet, it would be better not to attempt it. If you think you will probably cave in if he tries to control you with either anger or promises of instant reform, with threats of one awful outcome or another, then you're not ready for this level of challenge yet. I'll not pretend to you that this won't be one of the most painful experiences

you will ever face. I know I could never have done it without the assur-
ance of the Lord that I was acting in accordance with His purposes.

---

*I am not sure whether my marriage will survive my husband's
addiction, but I am coming to a place that as long as I have
the Savior and His love in my life, I will be all right. I hope
and pray that my husband can find the peace that I have
found by turning to the Savior, but I am no longer feeling like
I have to be the one to fix him. That is why Jesus Christ came.
Somehow, as I have focused on my relationship with the
Savior, I have become a new person. My relationship with my
husband is evolving and changing because I am different. Like
I said, I don't know where it will all end up but for the first
time in years I have hope. That is worth more than any
worldly treasure to me.*   *— Tanya*

In Conclusion: Angela's Story

*I knew it was time. I confronted my husband. That sounds very aggres-
sive, but it really wasn't. There wasn't a lot of yelling or screaming or
uncontrollable rage. He downplayed the situation. I remained firm in my
decision to have him move out. I wanted a husband who would walk with me
towards God or no husband at all. He asked for a bit of time so that he could
find a place to live, get a job, etc., to which I agreed.*

*After a few days, he started behaving as if everything were normal. I had
to remind him that I wanted him to move out. I felt so mean, but I had come
to the point of no return. Several times I had to repeat my request and he
ignored me. Just as I was getting to the point where I was no longer willing to
wait, my husband realized I was serious. His next tactic was to tell me that if
this was going to happen, he was going to do all he could to get our sealing
dissolved. (In my mind it already felt like our sealing was void because we
were not striving for a celestial marriage and covenants were not being kept.)
When I refused to back down from my stand, he had our bishop requesting*

that our sealing be cancelled since I was insisting that he move out. That is when the miracle began.

I don't know what was said in that conversation, but while he was talking to the bishop, something is his heart was touched and he realized that he needed to do some repenting. This much I do know: my prayer was answered in such a way that I knew I didn't have to walk alone. Looking back over the previous five years leading up to this moment, I could see that God had been walking with me every step of the way, providing me with experiences to help me gain strength, courage, and wisdom, so that I would be strong enough to take the steps I needed to take and finally get out of His way so that He could do His work.

The end result is that my husband was excommunicated, but that has given him freedom from his sins and the ability to truly repent. He has found light where there had been darkness for so long. Has this path been a breeze? No. We both still have old habits. I have fears, hurts, and anxieties to overcome, but now I can talk about my feelings openly with him and he is hearing me. I still rely upon the Lord very much and want to continue to do so forever. For a while I thought, what happens if he has a relapse? What if all of this is just for show? How will I handle that? The answer came that I needed to watch his attitude as he got back on course. Some days are not easy, but things are getting better.

We are still together and building a new relationship. I know this outcome might not be the same for everyone. Our stories are individual. You will know when it is time to either quit or continue forward. I know it is very difficult to decide, especially because of the children. Because I come from a broken home myself, I didn't want my kids to go through that, but then it finally got to the point where the present was more painful than the alternative (if that makes any sense). What would I advise others? I would advise you to continue working on your relationship with the Savior, grow closer to Him and lean on Him. Trust that He will always be there and that you can hear His whisperings.

---

1. *Alcoholics Anonymous*, 4th Edition. Hazelden Publishing, 108.

Chapter **13** *What If We Can't Reconcile?*

If you are seriously thinking of ending your marriage, we are sure you have been through a lot before coming to this critical point. There have been a lot of tears, a lot of interactions with your husband, and probably much counseling with friends, family members, counselors, and priesthood leaders. If you haven't had these discussions, we encourage you to do so before taking this next final step. Divorce is not to be approached lightly or in a fit of anger or without a great deal of prayerful effort to seek and receive the counsel that matters more than any other—the confirmation that comes from the Lord.

I spoke with our branch president yesterday. He told me I needed to pray about it and take it day-to-day. If in time my husband hasn't shown improvement or desire to stick with the 12-Step program I should then make my decision. Of course he didn't tell me what decision that should be, but I've found the support and strength to make that decision if the time should come. I am praying hard that this is the final time and that my husband truly does change, but I think it is time for me to get my chicks in a row and prepare in case he finds he doesn't want to change. — Betty

---

Colleen: The Only Source of Peace Equal to This Challenge

Phil and I have talked over this chapter and come to the conclusion that since his parents were devoted to each other their whole lives and he has never considered divorce in either of his own marriages, I need to do most of the sharing on this topic, based on my own experience. Before we begin, I hope you'll bear with me as I admit to you up front that composing the thoughts for this chapter has stalled me out for months. Living through a divorce is an experience that I would not wish on anyone. It brings me intense sorrow to admit that the need for active LDS women to be prepared in heart and mind for this possibility has increased in the twenty years since I faced it.

Finally, I knew it was time; this chapter had to be written. I had to stop wishing we could go straight to the chapter on rebuilding the marriage. That is the outcome I pray for in behalf of everyone reading this, but for some of you, reading this chapter will turn out to be necessary. I pray that each of you will seek and find that supernatural, illogical peace that only the Savior can give—a degree of peace that makes no sense considering that you're forced to entertain the possibility of divorce. It is, as the scripture puts it, the peace that "passeth all understanding."

> **And the peace of God, which passeth all understanding, shall keep your hearts and minds *through Christ Jesus* (Philippians 4:7, emphasis added).**

This is the kind of peace that I had to seek when I was facing the end of my first marriage. It is the kind of peace that no earthly source could give me. No amount of counseling, either from professional or priesthood sources or closest friends or loved ones, could ease the horrible pain and fear that I dealt with day and night. No, the relief I needed during those months and years was relief that only God could give. In the Savior's own words:

> **Peace I leave with you, my peace I give unto you: not as the world giveth... Let not your heart be troubled, neither let it be afraid (John 14:27).**

It is only with those words strengthening me that I can come to you through these written pages and try to share what it meant to me as a 100% committed and 110% active LDS woman to end a temple marriage in divorce. As I said earlier, it felt to me like a fate worse than death. I don't know if there has ever been a woman in the Church more determined than I was to never divorce. Not one of the "hard moments" (and there was an increasing number of them as the years went by) could tempt me to contemplate divorce. I wouldn't even allow the word to be on the radar of my mind. I was determined that I was going to make this one-and-only temple marriage work or die trying. I was not going to go back on my covenants.

I filled journal after journal with thoughts and feelings as I poured out my heart and soul to the Lord in prayerful writing, both during the years leading up to the choice and in the years afterward as I lived with the repercussions. How could this have happened? How did I get here? After all, a woman doesn't spend twenty-three years in a marriage and bear twelve children imagining that she would ever be divorced.

Facing the Unthinkable

> **Wherefore if thy hand or thy foot offend thee, cut them off, and cast them from thee: it is better for thee to enter into life halt or maimed, rather than having two hands or two feet to be cast into everlasting fire.**
>
> **And if thine eye offend thee, pluck it out, and cast it from thee: it is better for thee to enter into life with one eye, rather than having two eyes to be cast into hell fire (Matthew 18:8-9).**

The footnote to this verse in the Joseph Smith Translation indicates that the "hand" and "foot" refers to "friends" that expose you to evil, and that the "eye" refers to "they of [one's] own household."[1] The heartbreaking truth is that divorce may be the price you have to pay to have any hope of raising your children in a spirit of righteousness and to regain a feeling of personal respect and dignity in your own life. You may have to give up your dreams of an eternal marriage with the man you had believed you would remain married to forever.

A few years ago, I listened with compassion and empathy to a news story that was a living parable of what it was like for me to do all that I could to save my marriage, and then, finally to have it end.

It was in May 2003 that Aron Ralston was climbing alone in Blue John Canyon in southern Utah. Suddenly, an 800-pound boulder shifted, crushing his lower right arm and hand, and pinning him to the canyon wall. For six days, plagued with dehydration and hypothermia, he tried unsuccessfully to free himself from the huge boulder. When he at last concluded that he was on the verge of losing his life, Aron decided that if he wanted to live, he would have to do the unthinkable. He would have to amputate his own arm and hand, using the only tool he had with him—a cheap multi-tool knife blade! It was an unimaginable, nightmarish experience, but with the aid of a tourniquet he accomplished the task. Then, as if that were not enough, he had to rappel to the bottom of the cliff all alone. Eventually he found some campers who helped him until a search-and-rescue helicopter could airlift him to a hospital where surgeons and other experts could help him begin the long, horrendous task of recovery.

For me, my friends who stood by me while I went through the process of severing myself from the single greatest hope I had ever had in my life—a marriage for time and all eternity—were like those campers that helped Aron when he first stumbled out of the canyon, dehydrated, emaciated, and bloody. But like those campers, my friends could only do so much. It took the arrival of the helicopter and the surgeons at the hospital to help Aron fully recover.

For me, the equivalent of Aron's experience of being air-lifted and life-flighted to the hospital happened as I applied the principles of the Twelve Step program to this latest crisis in my life and allowed those principles to bring me into the presence of the greatest physician of all, even Jesus Christ. These same principles that had helped me deal with my first insurmountable challenge (my compulsive eating) led me once again through this otherwise unbearable challenge of ending my first marriage and becoming a single parent with eight children under eighteen years old still at home.

Aron is now fully recovered and is still climbing mountains. He is doing what we all must do with a tragedy if we are to live by the example our Savior has set: We must learn from it and let it give us experience—just as the Lord told Joseph Smith when he cried out to Him for rescue while he lay in the horrible conditions in Liberty Jail.[2]

Allowing Christ to Empower You to Do What Must Be Done

I offer the following words from President Ezra Taft Benson and from Moroni as testimony of the fact that it is totally appropriate and doctrinally sound for each of us to reach out to our Savior and to rely on Him to be the rock of our redemption and salvation if divorce becomes inevitable. They are among the most important counsel I ever received and thus the most important that I could pass on to you:

> **Establish a deep and abiding relationship with the Lord Jesus Christ. Know that He is there—always there. Reach out to Him. He does answer prayers. He does bring peace. He does give hope. In the words of the Psalmist, "He is my refuge and my fortress...in him will I trust" (Psalm 91:2). Study carefully the life of the Savior. He is our great exemplar.**
>
> **Make the scriptures your constant companion. Read daily from the Book of Mormon and receive of its strength and spiritual power.**
>
> **Realize your personal self-worth. Never demean yourself. Realize the strength of your inner self and that, with God's help, you "can do all things through Christ which strengtheneth [you]" (Philippians 4:13). Life does not begin only upon marriage (Ezra Taft Benson, "To the Single Adult Sisters of the Church," *Ensign*, Nov. 1988, 96).**

Here again, it was President Benson's constant testimony to the Saints that it was acceptable to seek **"a deep and abiding relationship with the Lord Jesus Christ"** that permitted me to do as Moroni had invited, to **"seek this Jesus of whom the prophets and apostles have written."**

> **And now, I would commend you to seek this Jesus of whom the prophets and apostles have written, that the grace of God the Father, and also the Lord Jesus Christ, and the Holy Ghost, which beareth record of them, may be and abide in you forever (Ether 12:41).**

Admittedly, even with the guidance of the Lord, it was the equivalent of a long, hard journey for me to allow my old dreams to die and to find new dreams. As we've discussed the various topics in earlier chapters, I've shared glimpses of what it was like to be married to my first husband. I've shared how hard I was on myself physically, emotionally, and even spiritually, trying to be and do whatever he wanted. It took a lot of humility on my part for me to wake up to the truth that I had put him in the place of the sun and the moon in my life, or to put it even more literally—I had made him my god.

One moment of recognition came as I sat in a recovery meeting focused on unhealthy eating and listened as another woman said she was so obsessed with weight that every morning of her life she stepped on the scale to see what kind of day she was going to have. I sat there in shock as the Spirit of Truth whispered into my mind that which I needed to hear, that I got up every morning and looked at my husband's face to see what kind of day I was going to have. It took several years of recovery meetings, scripture study, and journaling, but eventually I came to realize that I had been fearing man (a specific man) more than I feared (respected, honored, trusted) God.

As I continued to study the principles of recovery contained in the Twelve Steps, they helped me follow President Benson's counsel as cited earlier. Jesus became my nearest, dearest counselor and friend. The twelve true principles found within the Twelve Steps opened a channel of communication between me and the true and living God. I began to understand some things I hadn't been able to admit or to see in all the years I had been blinded by my fearful codependency.

What the Lord Testified to Me that Helped Set Me Free

I felt *and began to believe* how much my Heavenly Father and Jesus Christ and the Holy Spirit love me. I had longed to have my first husband love and cherish me, to never want to do anything to hurt me, but as the Spirit of Truth entered my heart, I realized it wasn't going to happen. Feeling the love of God (all three members of the Godhead) for me gave me a way to wake up and realize how devoid of love my marriage had become.

I felt God's testimony that I had done all I could possibly do to help my husband, and it was time for me to be released from the calling. Truly, that was the witness I felt. I saw that my marriage to this man was a calling given to me by God. It was a marriage that had pleased the Lord when it began. I had been called of God to be my husband's wife and helpmeet (to help him meet the measure of his creation by bearing his children and helping him fulfill his priesthood callings), but it was time for me to be released—and to be released honorably. I felt the witness of God that He would continue to do all He could for His son, but it would no longer be through me. I was released from being the Lord's instrument in my husband's behalf.

Obviously, this is not a testimony that you can get from anyone except Heavenly Father and the Savior, personally and directly. To fulfill your temple covenants, you should do all that you can to hang in there and keep trying until this witness comes into your own heart. When the release comes, it is accompanied by that peace **"which passeth all understanding"**[3] that (once again) only God can give.

It was made very plain to me through the Spirit's witness that it was not pleasing to my Father in Heaven that my children and I should continue to live in a state of spiritual starvation. By the time I surrendered to this most painful truth, I had already lost my eighteen-year-old daughter in an alcohol-related car accident. Each of my other children was struggling with one kind of problem or another. Even my older sons, who had already served missions and were young adults active in the Church, were deeply scarred by the atmosphere of tension and negativity they had grown up with in our home. I had often heard how damaging divorce can be to children, but I began to realize that nothing could be more damaging than for them to continue living in the secret sin that I had recently become aware of. (By this time I had discovered that their father's addiction had involved several of them in sexual behaviors.)

I felt the Lord's promise to me that He would lead me and any of my children who would go with me to a **"far better land [life] of promise."**

> **And now I say, is there not a type in this thing? For just as surely as this director did bring our fathers, by following its course, to the promised land, shall the words of Christ, if we follow their course, carry us beyond this vale of sorrow into a far better land of promise (Alma 37:45).**

In 1990 being divorced was virtually the same as having leprosy, especially in the community in which we lived. I was tempted to be terrified of what the future might hold for us financially and socially, but I kept feeling the irrational witness from the Spirit that all would be well. I had no certain prospects for what that "land" or better life would look like, I just knew that I had to do what Abraham, Lehi, and later Nephi had done: I had to end my association with the life and world I had always known and strike off into the unknown, trusting in the "words of Christ" to guide me.

You Don't Need to Fear Going on Alone

I have spoken with so many sisters who are convinced that without the presence of a man in their homes, their family did not have the blessing of the priesthood. When I was left alone with my children, I asked my home teacher for a blessing, and I believe the words he was given to share with me are equally true for every faithful LDS woman who finds herself in these circumstances. Through this good man, the Lord reassured me that as long as I exercised faith in the power of the Holy Priesthood, I could be sure that it would be effectual in blessing me and my children directly through the Spirit of the Lord dwelling in our home with us.

One of the most powerful ways to tune your heart and mind to the comfort and counsel that can come to you from your Elder Brother and Heavenly Father is to study and apply the principles of recovery in the Twelve Steps. Having this crisis come into your life is your opportunity to come to know the Holy Spirit, the Lord Jesus Christ, and your Father in Heaven like you have never known Them before.

Another way to open that channel of communication with God is to go to the temple as often as you can. While you are there and after you leave the temple, ponder deeply your covenants with God. These three perfected Men—your Heavenly Father, your Savior Jesus Christ, and the Holy Ghost—will never leave you or lead you astray. They love you beyond all understanding.

Just as the temple teaches, the Lord is waiting for you "at the veil," through the two gifts that are given to you as channels of revelation. One of those gifts is your own conscience or prayerful intuition, the Light of Christ. The other is the gift of the Holy Ghost. The Holy Spirit can connect you in heart (feelings) and in mind (thoughts) with the other two members of the Godhead. The Holy Ghost will whisper "the words of Christ" into your mind.

> **Angels speak by the power of the Holy Ghost; where-fore, they speak the words of Christ.** *Wherefore, I said unto you, feast upon the words of Christ; for behold, the words of Christ will tell you all things what ye should do* **(2 Nephi 32:3, emphasis added).**

And they did! The "words of Christ" (thoughts, impressions, guidance) came into my mind and began to tell me what to do. As I made decisions for my children and for myself, I felt like I had the most wonderful, respectful, peaceful partner shouldering the burdens and challenges with me. I found myself knowing by my own spiritual experiences what the Savior meant when He said, **"I will not leave you comfortless. I will come to you."**[4]

Seeking a Divorce Can Be an Inspired Act of Humility

It took five years of watching the ugliness and hatefulness in our home escalate before I could humble myself and admit that I could no longer bear the burden of trying to hold my marriage together. During those years, I begged my first husband to go to marriage counseling with me. On several occasions he went, but every time his participation would end when the therapist began to ask him to do some one-on-one sessions. It seemed that he was more than willing to sit through sessions that focused on what was wrong with me or what was wrong with our marriage (me), but not when the focus was on what he might be believing, thinking, or doing to contribute to our troubles.

I began to allow the thought of divorce to cross my mind only after watching years of effort to save the marriage fail over and over, while the disease and soul-sickness in our family system worsened. I was filled with the testimony of the Lord that I had to prepare for the unthinkable—for divorce. It was like I had lived with a cancer diagnosis for many years and thought I would be able to beat it, to have it go into permanent remission. I had thought I might be one of the people to miss the bullet or avoid the grim reaper, but it was becoming clearer and clearer that the situation was terminal.

We've all heard of times when a person is dying, but can't pass on until someone who loves them intensely surrenders to the inevitable and finally lets go. I had to surrender to the truth that no further amount of effort to save my marriage was going to revive it. I had to surrender to the truth that there wasn't a marriage to revive, that we had been living in a situation that was the equivalent of keeping a body alive on life-support. It was time to admit it. My oldest daughter was already dead and the rest of my children were acting out more and more frequently. They were earning the reputation of being troubled kids in our ward and people were beginning to express negative judgments toward them. It was increasingly obvious that, at least in my case, staying in the marriage, trying to hold the family together, was as deadly as forcing us to live in a house filled with toxic fumes.

At that point, I stopped refusing to face the possibility that our marriage was not going to make it. Still, I pled with the Lord to reveal His final word to me *personally* about divorce. After all, for the entire twenty-five years I had been a member of the Church, I had heard that it was a sign of gross selfishness to seek a divorce. I didn't think I was being selfish, but then maybe Satan had me twisting the truth. That was certainly what my first husband insisted I was doing.

I fasted. I went to the temple on my own. I sought counsel from the most faithful and wisest priesthood holders I knew, men who were like fathers and older brothers to me. I received priesthood blessings. I studied the scriptures and the teachings of the latter-day prophets. I prayed aloud several times a day, brought to my knees by this terrible burden. I wrote in my journal and kept a daily record of what was happening inside my heart and mind, as well as what I found in my studies. Today I am so grateful for those journal pages. As I go back and read them, it is very painful, but it is also *very* apparent that I did not come to divorce lightly or selfishly. It is because of that written record that I am able to retain in remembrance the fact that my choice to divorce was based on powerful personal revelation.

My decision was finally reached when, in a matter of a few weeks, the Lord led me to three situations that confirmed I was not being deceived in considering divorce. The first witness came when my bishop, with tears in his eyes, told me that he could not in good conscience counsel me to stay in my marriage. This moment came after another futile session of counseling with my husband and me. It had ended with my husband all but cursing the bishop for taking my side, then leaping to his feet and rushing out of the bishop's office in a rage. I felt the truth in my bishop's words pierce me, but I still needed at least one or two more witnesses for it to be firmly established in my heart.

The second witness came as I studied the scriptures, praying constantly to be shown the truth I needed to guide me. One morning the Lord showed me that while it was more pleasing to God that a man and woman marry for eternity, He also knew that some men's hearts might become hardened to the point that divorce would be necessary. He opened this to my understanding by first reminding me that when a prophet makes a pronouncement to the entire Church, we need to recognize his words as being the Lord's own words.[5] Then the Lord reminded me that it was Moses—indisputably a spokesman for God—that spoke for God when he introduced the possibility of divorce to the children of Israel.[6] Finally, the Lord led me to His own testimony concerning divorce, uttered when the Pharisees were questioning Him, seeking to catch Him in a falsehood: **"He saith unto them, Moses because of the hardness of your hearts suffered you to put away your wives: but from the beginning it was not so."**[7]

I put my head down and cried over these words. "Dear God," I prayed, "I don't want to be hard-hearted. I certainly don't feel hard-hearted. I feel *crushed*, like the olives in the olive-press. I feel broken-hearted almost beyond rescue." Like Alma, I found myself calling directly upon my Savior to deliver me, **"O Jesus, thou Son of God, have mercy on me."**[8]

The last witness came in the form of a statement by another prophet—this time a modern prophet, President Joseph F. Smith, who offered me the mercy for which I had pled:

> **If a man and woman should be joined together who are incompatible to each other it would be a mercy to them to be separated that they might have a chance to find other spirits that will be congenial to them. We may bind on earth and it will be bound in Heaven, and loose on earth and it will be loosed in Heaven (James R. Clark, comp., *Messages of the First Presidency of The Church of Jesus Christ of Latter-day Saints*, 4:327-332).**

While it is inevitable that there are people who would use the mercy President Smith (and the Lord through him) extended as license to justify divorce in order to satisfy their own selfish desire, to shirk responsibility, or to abandon a partner in order to pursue sin, this did not apply in my case. President Ezra Taft Benson once made the statement, **"The world would take people out of the slums. Christ takes the slums out of the people, and then they take themselves out of the slums."**[9] For me, his words perfectly expressed my motive for ending my marriage.

The choice of divorce was the best for everyone involved. It would be wrong for me to say that you need to do the same thing, but what is right for me to say is that Heavenly Father does love you. You are His daughter. He desires that you have happiness in this life. Through His Holy Spirit and because of the Atonement of His Son, our Savior, He will give you clarity of thought. He will guide you to the degree that you allow Him. He will raise up friends, give you courage, encircle you in His loving arms and infuse your very being with peace.

As far as how do you know? I asked myself that question many, many times over many years. I have been married for twenty-five years and it has been a roller coaster ride. No one can tell you when enough is enough...only the Lord. Go to Him in prayer, seek guidance from Him (as I'm sure you have already done). I was looking for someone to tell me when it was time, but no one [but the Lord] could. — Linda

Living with Your Family "After the Manner of Happiness"

Without exception or doubt, the principles and teachings of the restored gospel are the greatest source of counsel and comfort we can ever turn to in this time of trial. As I went through the divorce experience, there was one more application of gospel truth that saved my life: No matter what happens to my *mortal* family, even if it has been led into a period of challenge and turmoil by another family member's choices, *I still have a family*. I will always be a part of my Heavenly Father and Mother's family. I will always have a perfect Elder Brother who will be there for me 100%.

I held my children in my arms and bore my testimony of this truth to them, that we are part of a bigger family that will never be torn apart. We have a Father and a Mother in Heaven. We have the **"the Holy Priesthood, after the Order of the Son of God,"**[10] in our home. The blessings of that priesthood were not vested only in the person of the mortal man I married. Those blessings of the Melchizedek priesthood are symbolized by my temple covenants and also by the companionship of the Holy Ghost.

This, dear sisters, is what it means to have the miracle of the restored gospel of Jesus Christ in your life. It is right at your finger tips if you will turn your heart to God and lay hold upon the iron rod of His words—both in the scriptures and in your heart and mind. This is the legacy that no man can take from you and that no heartbreak can cancel. You can continue living in the midst of your Heavenly Family even if your ward family doesn't come through for you, even if your earthly family (parents and siblings) don't support you. You can live **"after the manner of happiness"**[11] in your own heart and home. Thus you can live encircled about in God's love and radiate a spirit of peace.

I'm not trying to whitewash the truth of how hard it is to go through the experience of a divorce or the fact that it takes most of us a long time to recover from this trauma. I wish I could say everything you need to hear about this subject, but I cannot. No one can. Nevertheless, if you will go forward prayerfully, you will be led to the counselors, the literature, and the support people who will be the instruments in the Lord's hands for you.

Once again—I can't testify of this enough—if you will stay close to the Lord through your own private, personal prayers and quiet times of journaling and meditating, He will fill you with the confidence and dignity you need to survive this season of your life and actually experience happiness again.

And now, my [beloved sister], remember, remember that it is upon the rock of our Redeemer, who is Christ, the Son of God, that ye must build your foundation; that when the devil shall send forth his mighty winds, yea, his shafts in the whirlwind, yea, when all his hail and his mighty storm shall beat upon you, it shall have no power over you to drag you down to the gulf of misery and endless wo, because of the rock upon which ye are built, which is a sure foundation, a foundation whereon if [we] build [we] cannot fall (Helaman 5:12).

I came to realize that I made the covenants and promises for myself. I have kept those covenants and have tried my best to live worthy of exaltation. I fall short, but I keep trying. I have wonderful children who are the joy of my life. They deserve to have a happy mother who doesn't carry around anger everywhere. I have made a mental choice to put myself, my relationship with the Savior, and my exaltation first. I believe with all my heart that if I do what I need to do, no blessing will be denied me. I feel happiness inside. I have reclaimed myself and what I want and believe.   *— Crystal*

One Last Reason You May Have to End Your Marriage

It is heart-breaking almost beyond words to address the subject matter that must be covered in this section, but it cannot be avoided. The reality we live with in the darkening shadows of the last days is that even among the Saints, horrendous sins are being perpetrated. These sins are so damaging to others that society has deemed them criminal. We have chosen to put the thoughts we have to share and the counsel we have to offer in an article in the Appendix entitled, "What If a Criminal Act Has Been Committed?"

If you feel the Spirit prompting you to face this painful possibility, we invite you to accept our reassurance that you are not alone in facing what needs to be done. I know the Lord will walk you through the legal processes and the mind-boggling fear and shame it will take to survive. I know because I have lived it.

1. Doctrine & Covenants 122:7.

2. Matthew 18:9, footnote "a" in the LDS Edition of the Bible.

3. Philippians 4:7.

4. John 14:18.

5. Doctrine & Covenants 1:38.

6. Deuteronomy 24:1, 3.

7. Matthew 19:8.

8. Alma 36:18.

9. Ezra Taft Benson, "Born of God," *Ensign*, July 1989, 4.

10. Doctrine & Covenants 107:3.

11. 2 Nephi 5:27.

Section 3

Embracing Your Common
Need for Recovery

Chapter **14** *Living Together in Recovery*

If, as you begin to seek your own recovery, you feel the witness of the Spirit that you need to stay in your marriage even if the circumstances are still hard, we would be glad to hear it. This is, in most cases, the first (and hopefully only) course of action for which you will need to find strength. We know that if you turn to the Lord, He will cause the burdensome issues in your present circumstances to be lightened so that you can rebuild the "happily ever after" you used to believe in.

We invite you to read again the story of the people who followed Alma, fleeing from King Noah as recorded in **Mosiah 24**. When they were captured and brought into slavery by the Lamanites, they cried to the Lord for deliverance. Interestingly, the Lord did not deliver them immediately, but He did something in the invisible realm of the spirit that lightened their burdens—so much so that they could not feel them.

> And I will also ease the burdens which are put upon your shoulders, that even you cannot feel them upon your backs, even while you are in bondage; and this will I do that ye may stand as witnesses for me hereafter, and that ye may know of a surety that I, the Lord God, do visit my people in their afflictions (Mosiah 24:14).

One Way or the Other, the Old Marriage Is Over

It is true that the journey you have been on is one of the most difficult you can know in this life. Your patience, your love, and maybe even your faith have been tried to the utmost. You haven't known how it would turn out. Perhaps you still do not. But maybe you can draw some strength and comfort from the Lord's promise in these words:

> **All things wherewith you have been afflicted shall work together for your good, and to my name's glory, saith the Lord (Doctrine & Covenants 98:3).**

If your marriage is going to survive the plague of sexual addiction, both of you will have to be willing to believe and trust in the words of that verse. It will take that kind of faith and commitment, just as much as if you were both starting over with new partners. Why? Because if both of you embrace the principles of recovery, you *will* become new people. Neither of you will be the same person who originally entered into marriage with each other. You will be wiser, more spiritually mature, as well as more certain in your testimony of Christ and of the principles of repentance and personal revelation. You will be humbled to realize just how close you came—or could have come—to losing the person most important to you, other than God.

One wonders how the seeking and finding of the Lord Jesus Christ can turn such exquisite sorrow and pain into exquisite joy, but we have the testimony of Alma that it can be done.

> **And oh, what joy, and what marvelous light I did behold; yea, *my soul was filled with joy as exceeding as was my pain!* Yea, I say unto you, my son, that there could be nothing so exquisite and so bitter as were my pains. ... on the other hand, there can be nothing so exquisite and sweet as was my joy (Alma 36:20–21, emphasis added).**

Most of us are familiar with the times during Christ's mortal ministry that He brought someone back from the dead. It is our testimony to you that Jesus' declaration, **"I am the resurrection, and the life,"**[1] is not only a statement of His power to bring individual people back to life, but it also declares what He can do for your marriage if invited by you. By accessing His atonement, the two of you together can be restored to faith in your marriage and to a deeper love for each other than you ever imagined possible before this crisis came along. In fact, your marriage can, like a muscle that has been stressed to the point of failure, actually heal and be stronger than before.

We pray that both of you will find that this crisis has become one of your greatest blessings as you have learned how important a partnership with Jesus is to your marriage. This new relationship with the Lord can and will heal and transform your marriage if you will allow it. As we said before: one way or the other, the old marriage is over.

Colleen: Seeking to Understand When and How to Forgive

Forgiveness. Is there any word in the whole vocabulary of recovery or of the gospel that holds more power to discourage you from thinking well of yourself? Everywhere you turn you hear people urging you to do what feels as impossible as holding your breath for half an hour. What if you can't forgive, *yet*? What if you can't imagine ever being at peace with what he did, or with how his infidelity has damaged you? What if it feels like a scar that you will carry forever? Or what if you've calmed down to the point that you can act as if nothing has happened as long as he behaves himself? Is it a lack of forgiveness to have your fear flare up in your heart and require you to deal with it so that you don't pretend you're okay when you're not?

Phil and I thought that this subject of forgiveness was a serious enough factor as to require its own discussion, so we'll revisit it in the next chapter, "Forgiveness *Is* a Miracle."

Making a New Start Built on Trust in God, Not in Man

In thinking about making a new start with your husband, you are probably asking, "Will I ever be able to trust him again?" Sadly, the loss of the trust you once had for your spouse is one of the deepest wounds you've sustained, and it may be one of the slowest to heal. One by one, your fears will have to be allowed to fade, but it takes time, just like it takes time for a scar to fade.

Without a doubt, the most important thing to remember about trust is that there is someone you can trust implicitly and that is our Savior, who also represents the Father to us. Our Lord is the one who will never let you down, the only one who is 100% trustworthy. He will lift the burden of addiction from your husband if your husband will let Him. He will lift the burden of doubt and fear from you, if you will let Him. Trusting the Lord will get you through those transition times while you are rebuilding your ability to trust in your husband.

It Is Not Your Job to Rebuild the Trust

The process of rebuilding a marriage after sexual addiction has taken its toll is virtually identical to rebuilding a wife's trust in her husband's fidelity to her, both physically and emotionally. You cannot rush this process. No amount of verbal reassurance will bring back trust. Talk does not restore trust.

Continuing good behavior over a long period of time is required. Sometimes an impatient husband will hurl the accusation at his wife, "You don't trust me!" as if the loss of her trust represents a failure on *her* part, as if trust were his right. Trust is not a birthright that we deserve just because we are on the planet. Trust is earned by our behavior and can very quickly be lost the same way. Remonstrations on a husband's part do nothing to restore his wife's trust in him. If anything, they undermine it further.

A husband who is complaining that his wife doesn't trust him is not focusing on the real problem—*his* trustworthiness. His unwillingness to admit this truth and to be patient with the time it takes for trust to be restored is a sign of his incomplete recovery. You don't have to trust him until you can honestly do so. It is not your job to rebuild the trust—that is *his* responsibility. It will most likely take a long time, so be patient with yourself and with him.

I have been lied to and hurt deeply by my husband. I still don't trust him, but that is okay for now. I love him with all my heart and as long as he keeps trying, I will stay with him.
— *Roseanne*

Together, we bear testimony that the Lord has visited both of us in our individual afflictions. He has eased our burdens and eventually, in His own way and in His own time, He has removed them. Do not be discouraged. Do not despair. Trust Him. Seek Him. Look unto Him to live each new day. He has not forgotten you. You can rely on that.

Trust Can Be Regained in Stages

Does this mean that a man must live a life of perfect abstinence before *any* measure of trust is restored? Are there stages of trust that can be regained along the way to a lasting abstinence? We think there are.

Very early in your husband's recovery, you may feel impressed by the Lord to trust your husband's sincerity. You can trust that he is genuinely trying and that his intentions are good. This degree of trust can be extended to your husband even before he has gained much abstinence.

The reality is that most men in the beginning stages of recovery will have several slips before consistent abstinence is achieved. Even so, your husband can demonstrate his sincerity by regularly attending Twelve Step meetings for support and by working with a sponsor. Most importantly, he can *and will* continue to do those things that will open his heart and mind to a *direct* relationship with God. He will make such activities as pondering the scriptures and keeping a recovery journal a daily priority. Seeing these things as a consistent part of his life can give you a measure of comfort and begin to restore your trust in the new man he is becoming.

Your husband's honesty will also represent progress in recovery, even if he has to honestly admit a slip. Before a person can become consistently abstinent, he must become consistently honest. Will your husband talk to you about his recovery, about where he is with things? Will he admit to you when he is struggling? It may be hard for you to hear, but his willingness to talk is a good sign.

Give him time. Give yourself time for trust to be restored. Turn to the Lord for the strength and comfort you will need during this period of recovery. Ask Him to show you the growth that needs to happen in you as you wait for your husband to recover.

Rebuilding the Marriage on the Rock of Personal Revelation

We are well aware that there are dozens of books and seminars available on marriage. A couple can spend anywhere from hundreds to thousands of dollars seeking counsel and guidance on how to salvage or rebuild their relationship. Most of the authors and counselors who have created the books and workshops and seminars mean well and have good things to share. Still, we hope with all our hearts that you will seek guidance first from the greatest marriage and family counselor possible, your Savior Jesus Christ.

We pray that by the time you have reached this point in your reading of this book, you will be persuaded that your Heavenly Father and your Savior are both as immediately available to you as a prayerful thought, whether you are kneeling, standing, walking, driving, at your desk, or doing the laundry. You can be thinking "unto the Lord" wherever you are.

We testify to you in the same spirit as did Alma. Let us liken his words to the purpose of our hearts in your behalf:

> **Therefore may God grant unto you** [our dear brothers and sisters]**, that ye may begin to exercise your faith unto repentance** [turning to God first for the power to turn away from wrongdoing]**, that ye begin to call upon**

> his holy name, that he would have mercy upon you;...
> **Humble yourselves** [before Him]**, and continue in
> prayer unto Him** [no matter where you are all through
> the day—not just once or twice a day in "formal" prayer]
> **...cry unto Him against the power of your enemies**
> [those who would entice you to sin]**. Cry unto Him
> against the devil** [who is at the root of all thoughts,
> words, or actions that would separate you from from God
> and from each other. Remember Satan] **who is an
> enemy to all righteousness...and when you do not cry
> unto the Lord, let your hearts be full, be drawn out in
> prayer unto him continually for your welfare, and also
> for the welfare of** [each other] **(Alma 34:17-27).**

You can trust that whether your prayers are uttered aloud or formed in your hearts, the Lord will answer with inspired thoughts and impressions. Thus His counsel will adapt any wisdom you glean from other sources to fit your circumstances and your marriage. We admonish you to seek Him before, during, and after any other counsel or therapy you may seek. Build your new marriage upon His word, upon the rock of personal revelation, and you can be sure it will weather any storm.

> **Therefore whosoever heareth these sayings of mine,
> and doeth them, I will liken him unto a wise man,
> which built his house upon a rock—**
>
> **And the rain descended, and the floods came, and the
> winds blew, and beat upon that house; and it fell not:
> for it was founded upon a rock (3 Nephi 14:24-25).**

Living Together "After the Manner of Happiness"

There are many books, CDs, and seminars that provide "to do" lists to change your behaviors and to demonstrate your love for each other. All of those acts are good, as far as they go, but we want to suggest that actions are just that—they are actions. They don't mean a thing if they aren't coming from a heart filled with respect, adoration, gratitude and mercy for each other, a heart filled with *God's* love for each other.

As we have lived together for nearly twelve years, we have discovered that we don't need to try to keep a million rules or guidelines in mind in order to live **"after the manner of happiness."**[2] Living by a list of guidelines can be compared to living by the letter of the law in marriage, instead of by the *spirit* of true marriage.

The spirit of marriage begins by heeding the prophetic counsel to "put God ahead of *everyone* else in our lives."[3] If you do this, you will learn that there are only a few principles needed to guide your marriage. You'll learn these principles by being exposed to and absorbing God's feelings of love for each of you. These principles will nurture the *spiritual* depths of your relationship. Loving, kind, thoughtful, deeply bonded actions will automatically result.

Here are the principles we feel the Lord has put into our hearts that make our marriage a joy to both of us.

Respect each other's individuality. Looking at the natural world tells us how much God values variety and differences. Someone once taught us a saying that we rehearse *frequently* to ourselves and each other: "Different isn't necessarily wrong. It's just different."

Think about how you feel in the presence of the perfect uniqueness of a newborn baby—especially your own. There is a feeling of awe, almost reverence, in your heart toward him or her. You are so aware of the *miracle* of this brand new human being.

The truth is, you and your husband are both still two of those miraculously unique beings. This is why a foundational principle for a genuine marriage is that both partners allow each other to have their own individuality. Respect and enjoy each other's differences. Trust that it is right to allow each other to have different tastes and different opinions.

Enjoy and cherish each other. Enjoying someone goes beyond accepting them. It goes beyond the usual meaning of loving them. Think about it. Being loved, as we often define it, means to care about someone. There's nothing shabby about that. But, if the feelings of God for us (each and every one of us, without exception) are an example, then we must understand that to love someone means that you *enjoy* them and *cherish* them.

Once again, it helps to come back to how we feel toward our own precious newborn babies. No one outgrows needing to feel that they are precious and beloved to another person. We invite you to think about how much it would mean if you both could sincerely say to each other, "I cherish you," or "I enjoy you so much."

Interact with respect for each other's feelings. The Lord reminds us that **"no power or influence"** can be maintained (even if we think we hold a position that deserves it) except **"by persuasion, by long-suffering, by gentleness and meekness, and by love unfeigned."**[4] If we feel a need to correct the other person, we do so in a gentle and thoughtful manner. It's also important to be considerate when discussing issues that the other person is sensitive about. Certainly, there should be no name calling of any kind.

Respect also includes avoiding sarcasm. Sarcasm is one of the most destructive influences in a relationship. The Latin root of the word, "sarcasm" means "to rip flesh." We need to remember that the sharpness we are counseled to use in reproving another[5] does *not* mean our words should be cutting, but rather that they should be clear and to the point.

Reveal your heart to each other without fear. While it is true that you need to respect each other's feelings, you must not refrain from telling the truth about your feelings. Communication between spouses is a form of interpersonal *revelation*. When we do not open our hearts to each other and offer to reveal ourselves, there is no relationship. If there was one thing and one thing only that we could say to you (other than stay connected to God), it would be *don't stop talking to each other.*

We were fascinated to learn some years ago that in ancient Hebrew—the language of Abraham, Isaac and Jacob—the words "covenant" and "conversation" were the same word![6] This under-standing reinforces how vital it is for a married and covenanted couple to keep talking, especially when things are difficult. If the conversation between us ceases to be free and easy and honest, then our covenant relationship is weakened.

Be connected with God. We assume, at this point, we don't need to say much more about how important it is to be connected to God. It is this message that we hope is plain and central from cover to cover in *From Heartache to Healing*.

Realizing the Addiction Wasn't the Only Problem

As recovery starts to unfold for both of you, and you find yourselves committed to forging a new marriage based on the Savior's love, you can be sure that the adversary will do everything he can to discourage you. You'll both need to remain determined to hang tough against Satan's continued attacks and to not become discouraged as other challenges and weaknesses arise and need to be dealt with.

Most addicts think their addiction is the main problem in their lives and that as soon as it is resolved, any other challenges will clear up automatically. Often, their spouses have the same expectation. Thus, many couples are dismayed when other problem behaviors continue or become more noticeable when the husband becomes "sober" from his sexual addiction. One wife of a sober alcoholic lamented, "He isn't drinking anymore, but he's still as mean as ever." In Alcoholics Anonymous, this is called being a "dry drunk," and in this, as in many other aspects of ongoing recovery, AA's Big Book lays the responsibility on the shoulders of the husband and father to humble himself.

> Yes, there is a long period of reconstruction ahead. We [addicts] must take the lead. A remorseful mumbling that we are sorry won't fill the bill at all. We ought to sit down with the family and frankly analyze the past as we now see it, being very careful not to criticize them (*Alcoholics Anonymous*, 4th Edition, p. 83).

This phenomenon of re-evaluation of one's character is a central part of the Twelve Step process. Recovery is not just about stopping the addictive acting out. It is about a mighty change of character, **"a mighty change of heart."**[7] This attitude of continued self-examination and repentance is not just applicable to addicts—it would bless all our lives.

Restarting a Sexual Relationship (If It Was Stopped)

True intimacy, especially sexual intimacy, must be based on mutual respect and consideration. Even as the marriage relationship improves, the sexual relationship will take time to heal. Years of dysfunction around sexuality need to be allowed to fade. The wife may be extremely cautious about future relations, having already been so deeply hurt. She may have post-traumatic stress reactions that need to be acknowledged. Both husband and wife must be prepared for love-making sessions to be interrupted in order to talk over each person's feelings. Often just acknowledging fear and reluctance can cause them to disappear.

While the world would define the power of sexual feelings in a man or woman as a purely biological drive, the "Proclamation on the Family"[8] makes it clear that the attraction between men and women actually predates our physical bodies. Our attraction for each other begins in the eternal depths of our being. Thus, the love between a husband and wife must be created spiritually first and then "clothed," so to speak, in physical gestures and intimacy.

This order of creating a true union between you as a married couple is in keeping with the principle of all creation as stated in the scriptures: **"First spiritual, secondly temporal, which is the beginning of my work."**[9] In a recovered and renewed marriage, sex needs to be the fruit of a great relationship, not the seed of it. Let your renewed physical relationship grow out of a deep spiritual and emotional connection. Let it flower from lots of empathy and sympathy for each other. Be best friends first, and lovers of each other's souls—not just each other's bodies.

Colleen: Starting Over—Focusing on Your Own Recovery

I am now in a marriage that is everything I've ever hoped for. I would have preferred to have had this happen with my first husband, the husband of my youth. That would have been my first choice and it was the motivation that kept me hanging in there for the twenty-three years I was married to him. After entering into the Twelve Step repentance process myself, I hoped and prayed for the last ten years of our marriage that my husband would come to admit his own need for a Savior, just as we are encouraged to do in **Ether 12:27.** He chose not to do that. He refused to admit he needed help. Eventually, the day came when I knew I could never wish or will or force him to recover.

I promise you, though, that you and your husband can rebuild the marriage you have if you will *both* embrace and apply the true principles that are represented in the Twelve Steps of recovery. I have seen hundreds of couples do just that.

Remember, the word "recovery," is absolutely synonymous with "repentance" and "redemption." Don't wait for your husband to take hold of these truths first. Go ahead and study and apply them for your own sake. In AA, they call this, "cleaning your own side of the sidewalk," or minding your own business. In the gospel it is stated very simply as working out our own salvation.[10]

1. John 11:25.

2. 2 Nephi 5:27.

3. Ezra Taft Benson, "The Great Commandment—Love the Lord," Ensign, May 1988, 4.

4. Doctrine & Covenants 121:41.

5. Doctrine & Covenants 121:43.

6. Brueggeman, Walter. The Psalms: The Life of Faith. Fortress Press, 1995, 154.

7. Alma 5:12-14.

8. "The Family: A Proclamation to the World," Ensign, November 1995, 102.

9. Doctrine & Covenants 29:32.

10. Mormon 9:27.

Chapter 15 *Forgiveness Is a Miracle*

Someone once joked that if you want to write an instant self-help best-seller, you need to write about either weight loss or forgiveness. That may sound funny to some people, but to most of the book-buying public it's a bitter kind of funny. For many of us, both weight loss and forgiveness are two of our most daunting challenges. Still, the books keep being written and published and bought and read.

Another reason for the constant flow of books on forgiveness may be that as long as we are mortal there will be injury and offense given and received between us all. If we think that we haven't caused others injury as we've gone through our lives, we are in denial (a nice way of saying we're lying to ourselves). Thankfully, it is true that most hurts are minor and the pain caused is temporary, easy to forgive and forget.

Sometimes, though, a hurt can knock us off balance and leave a deep bruise. In these instances, it takes time for the soul to completely absorb the damage and get back to normal. Most injuries heal and most people get over the experience and go back to living normally. But what about those injuries we sustain (or give) that are the equivalent of having a leg amputated or being stabbed through the heart? That is the symbolism the prophet Jacob used to describe the degree of injury a faithful wife suffers due to the infidelity of an unfaithful husband: **"many hearts died, pierced with deep wounds."**[1]

Obviously there is no place on earth to turn for complete restoration when such catastrophic injuries happen. While modern science can offer some pretty amazing substitutes for missing legs or a diseased heart, we don't think anyone would settle for those "make-do" fixes if there were a way to be made whole again. This is where we must examine and test our faithfulness in the power of Jesus Christ to actually restore to life that which feels dead. Will we come unto Him and seek in His companionship and counsel through the Holy Ghost the gift to do what we cannot imagine doing for ourselves? Can we let Him come into our hearts and change them so that we can have the burden of bitterness lifted right out of our souls? Can we be patient with Him and with ourselves as He takes the time to gently make us over in His Spirit so that we can begin to love as one with Him?

Taking the Time to Let Forgiveness Be Real

It is so important that forgiveness be allowed whatever time and patience it takes to become genuine. When it is pretended or rushed, forgiveness, like a shallow testimony, can wither almost instantly when exposed to future tests or stresses, just as the seed did in the Savior's parable:

> Some [seeds] **fell upon stony places, where they had not much earth: and forthwith they sprung up, because they had no deepness of earth:**
>
> **And when the sun was up, they were scorched; and because they had no root, they withered away (Matthew 13:5-6).**

We hope you'll feel the Lord's patience and longsuffering extended to you and that you'll know it is okay if you need some time to ponder and pray and work through to a place of sincere forgiveness. The process of becoming genuinely ready and able to forgive is a lot like having a delicate form of heart surgery that cannot be rushed, or like going through a long, drawn-out period of recuperation after a serious accident. Do not let anyone rush you or make you feel guilty for not being over it yet, even if it is your husband who keeps urging you.

It is not uncommon for a husband to become obsessed with obtaining his wife's forgiveness and to do everything from tearfully pleading with her to pressuring her with scriptures and modern prophets' quotes about her duty or obligation to forgive. His motivation is often an attempt to ease his conscience. It may also be that he wants to resolve the unfamiliar tension he feels when he sees you taking charge of your own feelings and not caving in to do or say what makes him feel better.

You don't have to feel guilty for not putting his needs ahead of your own at this point. Premature expressions of forgiveness don't really help either party. Premature forgiveness could be compared to a gift given **"grudgingly"** which **"profiteth nothing"** and is **"as if** [you] **retained the gift."**[2] In contrast, the release that comes with genuine forgiveness is a mutual gift from God to both of you, and is worth waiting for.

President James E. Faust of the First Presidency shared the following words of a sister whose marriage ended in a painful divorce in which she recounted her discovery that the Lord was not impatient with her as she worked through her feelings:

> **A sister who had been through a painful divorce wrote of her experience in drawing from the Atonement. She said: "I truly wanted to [forgive], but it was as if I had been commanded to do something of which I was simply incapable." Her bishop gave her some sound advice: "Keep a place in your heart for forgiveness, and when it comes, welcome it in." Many months passed as this struggle to forgive continued. She recalled: "During those long, prayerful moments... I tapped into a life-giving source of comfort from my loving Heavenly Father. I sense that He was not standing by glaring at me for not having accomplished forgiveness yet; rather he was sorrowing**

with me as I wept (James E. Faust, "The Atonement: Our Greatest Hope," *Ensign*, Nov 2001, 18).

It may help you to picture Heavenly Father and the Savior being this patient and kind when you remember that They taught Joseph Smith (and all of us along with Joseph) that **"no power or influence can or ought to be maintained *by virtue of the priesthood*, [but] *only* by persuasion, by long-suffering, by gentleness and meekness, and by love unfeigned; by kindness, and pure knowledge."**[3]

In other words, as the hymn puts it, "God will force no man [or woman] to heaven."[4]

Whether it's your husband that needs to have time to grasp the miracle of the Lord's gift of complete recovery, or you who needs time to progress toward the gift of complete forgiveness, God will be patient with you both.

God's Offer of Healing Never Runs Out, But Time May

The other side of the whole truth is that none of us can afford to procrastinate our healing and recovery. While God's offer to help and to heal us has no expiration date, earth life does. To forgive and to rebuild a marriage, to experience living together after the manner of happiness while still on this earth, requires both parties to still be on this earth. We all need to be doing whatever we can to contribute to our own healing—even if all we can do is to cry out to the Lord, as did Alma, and admit that crying out to Him is all we can do.[5]

After you start coming to the Lord, it will probably take some time for you to grasp what He wants to teach you. The Lord's offer to make you over into a person with the capacity to forgive your husband will take more than a one-time, quick-fix communication between you and the Lord. It will require you to let His Spirit enter into your heart and mind and teach you His ways over a period of time, the duration of which no one can predict.

Only He knows how long your training in godly love will take. He is hoping that you will let Him bring you further along on the path to becoming even as He is (and as our Father and Mother in Heaven are)—filled with infinite wisdom, mercy, compassion, and patience.

Colleen: The Lord Taught Me an Important Lesson of Forgiveness

In *He Did Deliver Me from Bondage*, I shared a dream through which the Lord taught me that if I want to enter into the gift of His Atonement, I need to be reconciled to those who have hurt me the most in mortality. I'd like to offer it to you as a parable that may be helpful in understanding how repentance and forgiveness are two sides of the same recovery process.

A Parable

One day I dreamed a dream in which I saw myself walking up a long, tree-lined lane, and though I was ragged and wounded and still using a crutch to steady myself, I was full of excitement. I had just entered into the last stretch in what had been a long and perilous journey home. Just over the next rise I knew my family was waiting to greet me. And when the breeze carried just right, I could hear the music and smell the feast at the great party they were preparing.

Suddenly I noticed that another figure was hobbling along just ahead of me. Whoever this poor soul was, I could tell that he was in at least as bad a shape as I was. But even with all his wounds, he had made it this far too. My heart went out to him in fellowship, and quickening my pace, I hurried to overtake him, calling out to him, "Brother, wait! Wait for me!"

He stopped and turned. My heart went chill as all feelings drained from it. I recognized his face. He had been my enemy, the very one who had inflicted the deepest wounds—wounds that had made my journey so slow and painful—wounds that I still bore unhealed. Not him! How could he be here too?

I halted my steps, unable to approach him any further, unwilling to say anything. As he called out, "Who's there? I can't see you," I realized that he was blind. Rather than answer his plaintive cry, I held my breath. Soon he turned, dejected, and shuffled on his way.

I didn't have far to follow him, for just ahead of us was a shining, glorious gate. The boundary that it marked was as definite as if it were guarding night from day. Even though the beauty of the country through which the lane passed was exquisite, what lay beyond the gate was beyond description, but not recognition. It was Home. Upon my seeing it, childhood memories seemed to flood my mind. Every path and byway was familiar to me. The longing to be there once more became an overwhelming ache within me. It caused me to totally forget my reluctance to approach my enemy, who was even now standing at the gatehouse, speaking to the Gatekeeper.

The gatekeeper had his back to me. Still I recognized Him immediately as my Lord and Good Shepherd, He who had carried me throughout much of my journey, ministering to my stubborn wounds. Just as He had promised, He employed no servant here. Still I could see only my enemy's face. There was light shining either from it or on it. I could not tell which. Suddenly I realized that his eyes were bright and clear, focused upon the face of the Gatekeeper. I realized he was not blind anymore! Then I noted how straight he stood. Eagerly I threw down my crutch and rushed forward. Maybe I too could be made whole!

Before I could take more than a step or two, I was suddenly aware of the Gatekeeper's words to my lifelong enemy. "There is only one last thing before you are ready to enter in, one last question I must ask."

My enemy! This person who had been responsible for my deepest wounds? He was about to enter in? The Gatekeeper continued, breaking through my shock, "Are you a friend to every man?"

Taking his gaze from the Gatekeeper's face, the man looked steadily into my eyes, and I knew that he was seeing me, really seeing me, for the first time. Somewhere inside I trembled. I had known all along that I would have to face the Lord to enter in, but my enemy?

His words pierced my soul. "I am willing to be," he said quietly. Healed and no longer blind, he loved me. Could I, still maimed and crippled as I was, say the same? Could I answer this one last question with an honest yes?

The Gatekeeper seemed to disappear from between us, though I knew He was near. Nothing stood between my enemy and me. He waited for my response with longing meekness in his eyes, unable to enter in without my approbation. And just as surely, I knew I could not enter in without him. My long-harbored resentment and bitterness, or all that lay beyond this last barrier—which would it be? Which would I choose? Why had I waited so long? How had I thought I could avoid this moment?

My first step toward him was still halting, as if crippled, but with each step my strength grew greater and greater. I could feel my wounds healing as I reached for his hands and then his embrace.

And as the dream ended, I saw us wrapped in more than each other's acceptance and forgiveness. The Gatekeeper and still another figure stood with us. With shining countenance the Gatekeeper turned to the other; and speaking my name in unison with that of my former adversary, He said, "Father, these are my friends." As I awoke from the dream, the last impression I had was hearing the voice of the Father, so long awaited, "Well done. You may both enter in."

I have come to understand by my own experience that Heavenly Father's purpose in putting us through this intense training course called mortality is to give us a chance to learn to repent and forgive.

This understanding has blessed Phil and me with the willingness to stop being bitter about what has happened to us along the way. Both of us have spent our fair share of time in our younger years doing the equivalent of being pouty little kids, sitting on our beds, doing our own "poor me" behaviors and refusing to (metaphorically speaking) come out of our rooms and get back into the game of life.

Finally, however, we have come to the point of finding ourselves ready to forgive God for being so dedicated to agency and imperfection in mortality. When you are ready, we can promise you that the Twelve Steps can be a powerful aid in understanding the magnitude of His love for you. For both of us, getting over our prideful self-pity and self-will was a big part of working through the steps. The steps taught us that neither of us had any power to do the super-human actions of leaving either addiction or anger and judgment behind. It was only by coming to God one humbling step at a time that we could find access to His power to do what we could not do on our own. We thank God every day that the steps helped us get past the road-blocks in our own characters that were keeping us from the Savior's offer of freedom and peace.

Colleen: Forgiveness Really Is a Miracle—His Miracle

Okay, hang on for what I'm going to share with you next. Some people who have read an early draft of this chapter think I'm going out on a limb to even try to explain the following experience I had with the scriptures. After all, it represents insights tailored specifically to me. But, then again, if there's even one person among you who may find relief from the heart-hardening, gut-wrenching idea that you have to manufacture or drum up the ability to forgive your husband on your own strength, I'm willing to share my story. I hope you will join your prayers with mine that the Spirit may help us reason together on this tender subject. Why? Because I'm going to share precious thoughts about what it meant to me to let go and to let the Lord take over.

I'm going to try to walk you through the scriptures and the way the Lord used them to lift the whole issue of forgiveness of my first husband off my shoulders and right out of my heart. I know that might seem unbelievable, considering that his acting out had taken the form of involving my children in sexual behaviors. I promise you, though, that the Lord truly did for me what I could not find the power to do for myself as I listened to Him open the scriptures to me.

It happened one day as I was "capturing" (writing prayerfully) the thoughts and feelings that came into my mind concerning my struggle with forgiveness. I opened the Topical Guide to "forgiveness" and began using various verses to anchor my writing. I was literally trying to hold to the iron rod, because I was tormented by uncertainty. Should I forgive? Was I uncharitable by withholding forgiveness? What did the Lord expect of me? How could I forgive what this man had done?

Suddenly, as I was in the midst of this intense labor, a light began to dawn in the eyes of my understanding. While I was reading in the Doctrine and Covenants, the Lord showed me why I couldn't find the gift of forgiveness for my husband in my own heart. It was not my gift to give; it was *His*.

I'll go through the verses I read one at a time and include the capturing I recorded in my journal as I sought to reveal my heart to the Lord and to trust Him to reveal His heart to me:

> **Wherefore, I say unto you, that ye ought to forgive one another; for he that forgiveth not his brother his trespasses standeth condemned before the Lord; for there remaineth in him the greater sin (Doctrine & Covenants 64:9).**

Dear Lord, I've heard the advice about how if I don't forgive this man, I will not be forgiven. It seems like one scripture after another says the same thing over and over. And now this one says that the "greater sin" lies in me! How can that be? How can there be a greater sin than what he has committed against his children, against me, or for that matter against Thee? I've tried and tried to forgive him. I know it's supposed to bless me to do so. I know that to hold on to judgment of him is only poisoning me. I can feel it. It twists my insides up. I have no peace. I've prayed for your power to come into my heart and give me the ability to extend the gift of forgiveness to him. Why won't you give me the power to forgive him?

I, the Lord, will forgive whom I will forgive, but of you it is required to forgive all men (Doctrine & Covenants 64:10).

*Dearest Colleen, I invite you to hear these verses in a spirit of mercy and love toward yourself. I invite you to realize that when I say, **"I, the Lord, will forgive whom I will forgive, but of you it is required to forgive all men,"** I am not cheating you out of anything. What I am trying to do is release you from the whole issue of sitting in judgment and forgiving or not forgiving your husband.*

And with the next verse, I continued to hear, through the Spirit, the Lord's invitation to me to be still and let Him be God:

And ye ought to say in your hearts—let God judge between me and thee, and reward thee according to thy deeds (Doctrine & Covenants 64:11).

In your heart, Colleen, all you need to do to be free of this insurmountable obstacle is admit that you are powerless to make sense of it and thus release the whole burden of judgment to me and say, "I will leave this with God. This is

His burden to carry—only He knows enough to judge right-
eously and reward (forgive or not) this person according to
his deeds." Colleen, I invite you to trust that I will do that.
Judging is a weight of spiritual maturity that you cannot bear.
I'll rescue you from it as soon as you're ready to let me.

Once I knew what it was I could do to be relieved, I found the power to go through with it. I found the humility to do as I had heard for years in recovery meetings, to "let go and let God." I was tired of trying. I was tired of beating myself up and thinking of myself as a spiteful, bad person who was unable to forgive. I was ready to let God be God, to let Him be in charge of judgment and forgiveness.

From that hour, the stress of trying to forgive my husband for his sins was swept away by the truth of the Lord's words to my heart. To this day, the miracle goes on. I can't say that I am not tempted sometimes to think a negative thought toward the man, but the temptation is fleeting and finds no lasting place in my mind or heart. When the Lord opened the words of those verses to my mind, I found the power to surrender to Him the right He earned in Gethsemane—to judge us all.

When Phil and I married, I was able to relinquish judgment toward his slippery months of early recovery. It was because I understood that judgment and forgiveness were the Lord's burden, and not mine, that I was able to stay out of the savior role with Phil when he slipped. When he came to me after his first slip and with a downcast countenance asked me to forgive him, I was able to say, "Phil, if you're asking if I'm okay with what's happened, my answer is no, not yet, but I'll get over it. I know not to take it personally. As to extending forgiveness to you so that you can feel everything's all right, you're asking the wrong person. Forgiveness isn't mine to give. It is God's and God's alone. You need to go to Him and work this out between you and Him."

Phil: What Colleen's Unexpected Response Did for Me

As I've explained before, in the years before I got into recovery while Kathy was still alive, my priorities were so messed up that I put my addiction ahead of pretty much everything else in my life. I risked losing everything dear to me by returning to acting out after each half-hearted effort at repentance.

That might seem like the *big* problem, but there was actually a worse one. It was the way I put Kathy's opinion (whether she was mad at me or forgiving of me) ahead of everyone else's, including God's. Her estimation of me was the only consideration in my mind when I was trying to repent. If she was upset with me, I was plunged into deep inner turmoil and couldn't rest until things got back to a positive feeling between us. Kathy was essentially my god and when she forgave me, things were wonderful again. Because hers was the judgment I was concerned about, when she was happy with me again, I felt as if I had repented, and my "god" had forgiven me. I didn't have to worry about what the God in Heaven thought.

I am so grateful that Colleen established the boundary that she did even before we got married. She refused to take on that "god" role, leaving me no other option but to face up to God with my sins. In doing this, Colleen wasn't being hard on me. She was simply directing me to the only one who could really help. Aside from the question of my comfort, my wife still has no power to forgive my sins or change my heart or my inner desires. She has no power to deliver me from temptation. Only Jesus Christ can do that. By directing me to Him, Colleen was doing the most valuable thing she could for my personal salvation.

1. Jacob 2:35.

2. Moroni 7:6, 8.

3. Doctrine and Covenants 121:41, emphasis added.

4. "Know This, That Every Soul is Free," *Hymns*, 240.

5. Alma 36:18.

16 A Wife's Twelve Steps

We should gather all the good and true principles in the world and treasure them up, or we shall not come out true "Mormons." — Joseph Smith[1]

I want to say to my friends that we believe in all good. If you can find a truth in heaven, earth or hell, it belongs to our doctrine. We believe it; it is ours; we claim it. — Brigham Young[2]

Have you been to any Twelve Step meetings yet? Do you still wonder what's so special and amazing about these Twelve Steps? Where did they come from? Who made them up? Did you know that the Church has adopted them as the official model of recovery both for those who are the addicted family members *and* for those who are the loved ones of the addicts? Did you know that for decades there have been LDS prophets and apostles who have recognized the power of the Twelve Step program to change hearts and transform lives?

Elder Matthew Cowley, who served in the Quorum of the Twelve Apostles from 1945 until his death in 1953, was so convinced of the Twelve Step program's value and power that he spoke of Alcoholics Anonymous (AA) in many conference addresses. Here are a few statements that illustrate Elder Cowley's admiration for the program of

AA—the original recovery program that introduced the Twelve Steps to the world:

> Sometimes our own people get the idea that AA is a religion. That if you join AA you may be taken out of your own Church. Oh, no. No, when a Mormon joins AA, he becomes the best Mormon he has been for many years....I've learned from these men that there isn't a man living who isn't greater than his sins, who isn't greater than his weaknesses (Elder Matthew Cowley, *Matthew Cowley Speaks*, 1954, pp. 212-219).

> I like to attend the Alcoholics Anonymous meetings. ... They do a great work....If we can just work these programs out right, we can accomplish almost anything....I am one of their head members...They bring into my heart a spirit of humility and a spirit of sincerity (Henry A. Smith, *Matthew Cowley: Man of Faith*, Bookcraft, 1968, p149, 151).[3]

In the nearly sixty years since Elder Cowley's inspired attitude of positive regard for the AA program, many other LDS leaders and members have recognized the harmony between the principles in the steps and the gospel of Jesus Christ. This harmony doesn't come as a surprise when we understand that the founders of AA took their original ideas from the New Testament book of James (the same book that inspired Joseph Smith to seek a direct answer from God when he went into the Sacred Grove in 1820) and from the Savior's Sermon on the Mount. AA's original formation was grounded squarely on Christian principles.

Amazingly, over the last twenty years the Lord has opened a way for us in the LDS community to "work these programs out right," as Elder Cowley put it, and to gather the true principles in the steps and "treasure them up" as the Prophet Joseph Smith invited us to do.

Colleen: One of the First LDS Twelve Step Study Guides

Within the LDS community, awareness of the Twelve Steps' harmony with the teachings of the restored gospel really took off when in 1995 the LDS Family Services pilot program for addiction recovery adopted *He Did Deliver Me from Bondage* as a temporary study guide. This book contains a chapter on each step and daily Book of Mormon study exercises that expand the reader's understanding of both the steps and the gospel principles with which they correlate.

Written from my perspective as a woman who has dealt with my own addiction and as a family member of addicted loved ones, the book testifies of how the steps helped me to access the Atonement of Christ. Over the next ten years, *He Did Deliver Me from Bondage* became the official study guide of the Family Services rapidly growing program. We would highly recommend that you make a serious effort to follow the Book of Mormon study and scripture-guided writing exercises offered in *He Did Deliver Me from Bondage*.

He Did Deliver Me from Bondage was retired from the Family Services program when the current book, *A Guide to Addiction Recovery and Healing*, was introduced. (Please see the Resources section in the Appendix for information about how to download all the chapters from *He Did Deliver Me from Bondage* from Windhaven Publishing free of charge. You will also find the URL for a free download of the current ARP guide on the same list.)

LDS Twelve Step Recovery—Support for Addicts and Loved Ones

Today there are numerous online forums and blogs where LDS members dealing with addiction can go to share their thoughts and feelings, but we know of only two programs that offer meetings as support to addicts and loved ones: the LDS Family Services Addiction Recovery Program (ARP) and the Heart t' Heart program. (Please see the Resources section in the Appendix for URLs to and other contact information for both of these programs.)

Many people think that Heart t' Heart is a copy-cat program of ARP. Nothing could be further from the truth. In reality, Heart t' Heart preceded ARP and was one of several LDS Twelve Step programs that ARP drew upon in creating their program. While the other programs chose to be absorbed into the ARP effort (since they were specifically alcohol and drug addiction recovery programs, as was ARP at first), Heart t' Heart chose to remain autonomous. Its hope and intention was to continue as an LDS community resource that would complement and support the Family Services ARP efforts.

At the current time Heart t' Heart does this by providing a website where addicts and their loved ones can find fellowship with other faithful, active LDS members in live online meetings and phone conference call meetings. Because these meetings are long-distance, they offer you complete anonymity.

Heart t' Heart also offers the opportunity to create local, face-to-face meetings where it is not yet feasible for an ARP group to form. Such meetings are required to register with the Heart t' Heart General Service Board and are only added to Heart t' Heart's official meeting list if they keep LDS standards and use only approved recovery literature as their study and discussion materials.

We feel that between the ARP program and the Heart t' Heart program, there is much instruction and support for LDS members seeking to learn and implement the principles of recovery found in the Twelve Steps. We highly recommend both programs.

We are also excited that LDS Family Services is currently working on study guide materials tailored specifically to family and friends of addicted people, even though the time frame for distribution of these materials has not been announced. While the lessons will not be aimed specifically at wives with sexually addicted husbands, it will be a great resource for you since the principles of recovery are truly universal. Meanwhile, we hope that *From Heartache to Healing* and *He Did Deliver Me from Bondage* can be of help to you on your own recovery journey.

Colleen: The Twelve Steps as They Apply to Wives

As you go to the websites we've provided in the Appendix, you will find the Twelve Steps paraphrased in a variety of ways. I have to admit that I'm prejudiced to the version that is in He Did Deliver Me from Bondage. These are also the official steps of the Heart t' Heart program, because they include the words of the Book of Mormon. (See Appendix page 208.)

I've created a personalized version to express what I, as a wife of a sexually addicted man, had to learn from each step.

Step 1:   I admitted that, ultimately, there is absolutely nothing I can do about my husband's addiction or his use of his agency, and that there is only one salvation I can work out—my own.

Step 2:   I became willing to believe that Heavenly Father sent His Son Jesus Christ to be my own personal Savior, and that as I come unto Him and seek to become as close to Him as I can, I will find comfort and counsel that will carry me through whatever I have to face.

Step 3:   I made the decision to trust God in all things, including the challenging experiences brought into my life through my husband's choices.

Step 4:   I made a fearless and thorough written inventory of my own past behaviors that contributed to my current challenges and the mistaken beliefs I held that caused me behave in ways that hurt either myself or others.

Step 5:   I admitted my past beliefs and behavior patterns to the Lord, to myself, and to another human being, and sought to understand how my beliefs were grounded in my own mortal tendencies to indulge in self-pity, self-will or self-righteousness—and sometimes all three.

Step 6:   I went through a period of time when I thought that I could change my own beliefs through my own willpower or by some means other than God, but all my efforts failed and I eventually surrendered to the truth that only He could change my heart.

Step 7:   I began to seek the Spirit of the Lord for my own healing, asking Him to change my heart and my character so I might find His peace and enter into His rest—no matter what others might choose.

Step 8:   I made a list of all the persons I had harmed in the past with my negative ways of thinking and acting, desiring to make amends and offer a confession and an apology however and wherever I could.

Step 9:   I made amends wherever possible, either in person or in writing, except when to do so would cause the other person further injury.

Step 10:   I continued to take a personal inventory from day to day and event to event, in order to honestly face my own wrongdoing in each current situation, so that I could promptly see and admit it, thus remaining always in a state of humility and repentance.

Step 11:   I sought through prayer and journaling to improve my consciousness of God's presence in my life and of His words to my mind and heart in order to stay in tune with His will for me and gain from Him the grace (power) to follow Him in all things.

Step 12:   Having experienced a greater degree of spirituality and personal connection to God through acting on these principles, I became willing to bear testimony of His living reality in my own life, so that others might be persuaded to come to know the Savior and to enter into the peace He offers us all.

My husband started going to 12 step meetings before I did. I was not willing to go because I thought it was his problem and he needed to deal with it. At the same time I was wanting things to change. Deep down I was not happy and was afraid that I would be unhappy for eternity. I prayed with all my heart that things would change. I thought it was my husband that really needed the change, but God blessed me with trials that brought me to my knees. I realized that I needed to recover. I needed a program of spiritual growth. I needed help to be restored to peace and serenity. That is when I began my journey. I found a good sponsor, took all 12 steps and felt of Christ's redeeming power for my life. When my husband saw that I had truly changed, he said, 'I want to do what you did.' And he did.   — Amy

Phil: Gratitude for My Wife's Understanding of the Twelve Steps

As I have related before, I first learned about the Twelve Steps from my first wife, Kathy, as she applied them in her life through her participation in Overeaters Anonymous. I saw right away that they were true principles. I regret that it took me almost twenty years to apply them to myself and my addiction to pornography.

However, even before I used the Steps for my own recovery, I was blessed by them, first as I shared the truth of my addiction with Kathy, and later when I married Colleen. Both Kathy and Colleen responded in the most appropriate way possible when I told them of my struggles and slips. They didn't overreact, but they didn't minimize the pain I was causing them, either. They didn't take responsibility for my addiction or my recovery. In short, they tended to their own recovery and let (expected) me to tend to mine.

Kathy and I learned so much from Colleen when we attended Heart t' Heart meetings in her home. I think that what Kathy learned from Colleen deepened her relationship with our Savior and put the finishing touches on her preparation to finish her mortal mission. As I had so much farther to go, I am immensely grateful for the years I have had since then with Colleen. She has continued to apply the principles in the Twelve Steps in her life, which has blessed me and our relationship immeasurably.

The simple restatement of the components of repentance found in the steps has been a touchstone that Colleen and I have turned to again and again in working out our challenges and our relationship with each other. I have heard the Twelve Steps called "Repentance for Dummies," but it would be better to say they are a course in applying the Atonement of Jesus Christ to the everyday problems of our lives. I am so grateful to my Savior and to the women who have taught me these principles.

1. Joseph Fielding Smith, *Teachings of the Prophet Joseph Smith*, p. 316,

2. Brigham Young, *Journal of Discourses*, 13:335.

3. Henry A. Smith, *Matthew Cowley: Man of Faith*. Bookcraft, 1968. Pages 146-151 of this book explain thoroughly how much Elder Cowley supported and encouraged the AA program's way of helping people overcome their addiction.

17 *The Tools Are for Both of You*

So what happens when a husband gets into a "recovery program"? Some of you already know. He goes to a lot of meetings. He reads and writes a lot. He's on the phone a lot with other people who are also in the program. You'd almost think he was back in college or some other intensive training program.

Well, you know what? He is! No, really! Picture what it would be like if he were in grad school or training for a special mission with the military. You wouldn't expect it to be a casual thing, would you? You'd expect it to be pretty intense. That's the way recovery is too—if a person is taking it seriously.

Seventy-five years ago, when the first hundred men began to find recovery from their addiction to alcohol through the Alcoholics Anonymous program, their wives found themselves facing the same dilemma as you are facing now. What do *you* do while your husband is focused on learning this new way of life that promises him a future free from addiction?

A number of those early wives got together and decided to do some recovering (learning and growing) of their own. They started holding meetings and studying the Twelve Steps for their own sake. They started sharing their experiences. Before long, they began to find their own recovery, strength and hope. Thus, Al-Anon was born and became a companion program for the companions of the recovering men in AA.

We hope that by now you are thinking seriously of pursuing your own recovery program, too. Trusting that the thought has at least crossed your mind—since you've hung in with us this long—we'd like to introduce you to the "tools" of recovery. They're called tools because they are things that a person can put into action, things a person can *do*, to help move their recovery forward.

To use a gospel expression, the tools are the "good works" of the recovery program. We must always remember, though, that the tools will simply be one more thing on our "to do" lists if we do not allow them to bring us to a personal inner life—to a *spiritual* experience that will awaken us to God as our nearest and dearest loved one.

Someone once said that a person can either use these tools like old-fashioned hand tools—twisting the screw-driver or swinging the hammer by their own puny power—or they can use them like *power* tools, letting God provide the power. When we allow the tools to connect us to Christ, who then blesses us with recovery, they become powerful indeed.

> *The tools are nothing but more busy work unless I'm using them as opportunities to look unto the Lord—to seek and see His love flowing to me through these various channels. If I'm sitting in a meeting, for example, and I am seeing and hearing only the faces and voices of the people around me and I am not connecting, seeking, looking (in the silent, private places within my heart and mind) toward my Heavenly Father and my Savior Jesus Christ, then I am not activating the real power of the truth that is available to me.* — Cindy

It is not through our "works" that we are healed; it is through the mighty change of heart that only the Lord can bring to pass. Our "works"—using the tools consistently and persistently—demonstrate to Heavenly Father and the Savior that we are willing to be free, whether it be from our addiction or our codependency. Demonstrating our willingness to change and to be healed calls down the blessings and powers of heaven.

It has been our observation from years of using the tools ourselves and helping others learn to use them, that they can be divided into two categories. There are those tools that help strengthen a person from the outside by offering them external support. There are those tools that strengthen a person from the inside, helping to build their personal internal connection directly to God.

External Tools: Ways the Lord Provides Support through Others

- Twelve Step support meetings

- Twelve Step websites, online meetings, forums, and blogs

- Telephoning

- Sponsoring

- Service

- Professional counseling

Internal Tools: Practices that Bring Us into Contact with the Lord

- Literature, including scriptures

- Music

- Writing

- Praying and Pondering (Meditating)

- Fasting, including partial fasts

You may have already started using some of these tools, but then again, maybe the whole idea of recovery is new to you. Maybe you're still trying to absorb why it is your husband has to be so caught up in all the new busyness of recovery. We'd like to go through the tools, one by one, and give you a basic look at each one—because the tools are for you too.

External Tools

First we'll take a look at the *external* tools. These are the ones that the Lord uses to offer us support through other people. If we remember that He is the one who is offering us support through others, these experiences can have a lot of spiritual power.

Twelve Step Support Meetings

It is always a little scary to go to a meeting you don't know much about, especially when it deals with serious, even heart-rending problems. Twelve Step meetings are not like encounter groups or other organizations that tear you down before trying to build you up. No one is required to embarrass themselves in front of the group. Each person is there for their own growth and learning. Members of the group are prohibited from giving advice. It is a safe, low-key environment where you can come and share only as much as you need or want to share. You are welcomed by others who gather to share their experiences and the strength and hope they are beginning to feel in recovery.

At the current time, there are only two specifically LDS organizations offering support group meetings. One is the LDS Family Services Addiction Recovery Program (ARP) and the other is Heart t' Heart. While Heart t' Heart continues to exist as a complementary program to ARP, its intent is to fill in wherever ARP groups have not yet been implemented. Heart t' Heart meetings can also provide additional anonymous support in areas where LDS members have a need or desire for more opportunities to meet in an LDS recovery environment.

It is an amazing experience to be in these meetings. Hearing the stories of others who share similar challenges can be uplifting and inspiring. You will come to understand that while there may be unique aspects to your situation, you are not alone in this struggle. Other women are facing the same issues, feeling many of the same fears. As you listen to the way others are coping with these same feelings and reactions you are experiencing, you will find hope and help.

LDS Twelve Step meetings are places where you have the chance to bring your specific problem and pain into an atmosphere of shared faith in the principles of repentance and redemption. These meetings are usually very spiritual as people share their testimonies about the core concept of our religion—the Atonement of Jesus Christ—and how accessing His power has brought miraculous changes in their hearts and minds that are gradually being implemented in their lives.

Twelve Step Websites, Online Meetings, Forums, and Blogs

Many non-LDS Twelve Step fellowships offer online and telephone meetings, but at the time of this printing the only LDS program offering long-distance fellowship and support is Heart t' Heart. Taking advantage of these online meetings can offers several benefits. First, they are available to you from your own home if you have an internet connection or telephone. Second, they are completely anonymous. (See "Resources" in the Appendix for the URL to Heart t' Heart's website where online and long-distance telephone meetings are listed.)

There are many forums and blogs online where the spouse of an addicted loved one can find support and exchange experiences with others. Some of these sites are specifically for LDS members. Heart t' Heart and Windhaven Publishing websites both provide forums that are securely grounded in LDS principles. Other blogs, forums and live chatrooms need to be approached with caution because they are not always focused on recovery. Sometimes they are dominated by a spirit of negativity and self-pity. Because of that, we'd like to offer the following suggestions in choosing an online forum in which to participate.

First, is the forum focused on working toward healing and recovery? Some people assume that expressing the hurt, anger, and shame they feel is the same as working through these emotions. Unfortunately that isn't true. Sometimes people are looking for allies to agree with them rather than looking for a solution. It is very possible to get stuck in a rut of self-pity or bitterness and confusion. Second, is the forum focused on

Christ and healing through His Atonement? As we have stated over and over in this book, our Savior is the only One who has the power to heal us. All of our recovery efforts need to be centered in Him.

Telephoning

At both ARP meetings and Heart t' Heart meetings, you may exchange phone numbers with other sisters if you wish, so that you can reach out to others between meetings to share hard moments as well as hopeful ones. These calls are usually kept to just a few minutes and are meant to help both parties feel strengthened in their recovery program.

Once again, like in your online connections with others, it is important that you be willing to call someone who understands the road to recovery rather than to talk with someone who will only commiserate with your complaints. An impromptu phone call can be like a meeting between meetings when the person we are talking to is also working a recovery program. When we have more time to spend on a call, it is suggested that we use this opportunity to read and discuss recovery literature with the person we've called. This keeps our sharing focused on the principles that will bless us.

Sponsoring

We believe that it is essential that you eventually work one-on-one with another person who has significant Twelve Step experience. In ARP groups, this person is referred to as a "support person." In most Twelve Step organizations, including Heart t' Heart, such a person is called a "sponsor." In either case, the idea is the same—that it is good to have someone to call with whom we can share our progress and study the steps. While working with a sponsor is a very helpful experience for the addict, it can be equally important for the wife.

I know I need to stop the cycle of obsessing, to focus on what I can change, let go of those things I can't change, and find the strength to know the difference! Thank you, dear friend, for sharing with me. It seems silly to find strength in knowing that someone else suffers as I do, but I appreciate your willing-ness to share. ...the hardest part in this whole battle is not the thought of losing my husband, but that I feel like I lost my best friend. I hope that I can find it within myself to strengthen others rather than just wallow in my own self-pity. — Ann

It is important to remember that even in a sponsoring relationship, the sponsor is not there to be a counselor or to give pointed advice. Each of us must exercise and develop our own personal channel of communication with the Lord so our answers will be our own. That is the most important counsel any sponsor can give those they are helping—to encourage them to study the steps, to use the tools, and to turn to the Lord to receive their own personalized guidance.

Service

The tool of service is virtually identical with the concept taught in church meetings. It has been a tool in Twelve Step recovery since the very beginning when Bill Wilson, the founder of AA, discovered that to keep his sobriety, he had to be willing to "carry the message of recovery," and to do all that he could to help other people get sober.

In Twelve Step programs, there are many opportunities to serve, such as coming early to help set up the meeting room and eventually to serve as a sponsor after you've had some time in the program yourself. It is often said that the most basic service we give each other in recovery meetings is just to come and fill a chair. Even if we don't say anything, we are giving service to others by being in the meeting and listening to the sharing.

Professional Counseling

One of the hallmarks of a true Twelve Step program is that, like the Church, there are no professional ministers or counselors to administer its services. Thus, you will not find any "professional" Twelve Step help.

Fortunately, though, there are professional counselors who understand and include the Twelve Steps as a resource for their clients.

If, as you pray, you receive a strong impression to include profes-sional counseling in your recovery program, we hope you will be able to find a counselor who respects the Twelve Step program. Unfortunately there are some who do not, mainly because the counselor does not value the spiritual, God-oriented approach on which the Twelve Step program is based. What is really exciting is that since the LDS Family Services ARP has started using the Twelve Step format, there are more and more LDS counselors recognizing the value of the Twelve Steps as a curriculum of healing.

We urge you to seek counselors who follow Christ and encourage others to do the same. If you choose to seek the advice of a counselor, find one who will listen to the Spirit in counseling you and who does not rely solely on his or her own wisdom. It is important that we remember the advice that Alma gave his people:

> **Trust no one to be your teacher nor your minister, except he be a man of God, walking in his ways and keeping his commandments (Mosiah 23:14).**

Internal Tools

As much as it helps to attend meetings, work with a sponsor, and use the other external tools, we believe the most important work of recovery, for both the addict and the spouse, happens spiritually as a person uses the following internal tools.

Literature

Studying literature in recovery work is more than reading. It includes taking time to listen to what the Spirit may want to teach you as you read. It includes taking time to slow down, to really absorb and to prayerfully think about how what you're reading applies to you. Doing this can turn the author's ideas into one half of a conversation, creating a dialogue instead of a monologue. That is why keeping a recovery journal where you record what you are studying and your response to it is such a powerful companion tool to reading. (See "Capturing" on page 205 in the Appendix.)

Scriptures. We know we may sound like the proverbial broken record on several points as we've shared with you throughout this book. This is one theme that cannot be repeated enough: *Of all the recovery literature you can study, the Book of Mormon is the most powerful.* It is a book that is *all* about people getting into situations they couldn't get themselves out of without coming unto Christ. That is why it is subtitled, "Another Testament of Jesus Christ." This great book was provided for us to convert the world to the Savior's true Church and to convert the members of His true Church to *Him.*

Twelve Step literature from other fellowships. In the years since Alcoholics Anonymous began, dozens of other recovery programs have sprung into existence. Most of the well-established programs offer literature created specifically for their particular challenge. Much of this literature can be helpful no matter which addiction you or your spouse are facing.

You will also find literature especially for the loved ones of addicts in S-Anon, Al-Anon, and Co-DA (Codependents Anonymous). While literature from these programs is not oriented to any one religious tradition, they all include powerful testimonies that harmonize with the prophet Mormon's words:

> But behold, that which is of God inviteth and enticeth
> to do good continually; wherefore, every thing which
> inviteth and enticeth to do good, and to love God, and
> to serve him, is inspired of God (Moroni 7:13).

In the last twenty years Twelve Step literature has been published specifically for the LDS community. Producing LDS recovery literature has been the mission of Windhaven Publishing since 1989, when Colleen began printing copies of *He Did Deliver Me from Bondage* at the local photocopy shop. Sixteen years later, in 2005, *A Guide to Addiction*

Recovery and Healing was published by the Church. Both of these books include scripture-guided writing exercises that are powerful tools to help you study and internalize the principles in the Twelve Steps.

Do you have the Twelve Step workbook? It really let me know my part in the whole thing—mainly to look to the Lord and be fearlessly introspective. I've tried many things including teaching my husband what he "should do." The best thing I've done is to work on my personal relationship with the Savior and have faith that the transformation will come in my life.

— Olivia

LDS Church Resources. The Church has a variety of resources published both in print and online. The Church website, *Combating Pornography*, contains a comprehensive listing of resources for addicts, spouses, parents, youth and Church leaders. (See "References" in the Appendix for the URL to this website.)

Music

Music can often put us in tune with the Spirit when nothing else can touch our hearts. Hymns, Christian music, classical pieces and other inspiring music can invite peace into our hearts and homes.

We agree whole-heartedly with the statement about music in the Heart t' Heart pamphlet on tools:

> Music is a powerful way to speak God's language, to praise Him and to express our deepest feelings to God and to others. ... Listening to inspiring music is both comforting and healing to our souls. This is especially true of the hymns. In the 1985 LDS Church hymn book, we are reminded that 'hymns invite the Spirit of the Lord...comfort the weary and console the mourning, and inspire us to endure to the end' (ix). [1]

Journal and Recovery Writing

Neither of us can recommend a tool that has helped us more than the tool of writing. Whether you choose to use inexpensive spiral notebooks in which you can write thoughts and feelings that you would rather destroy than keep, or you use a fancier bound journal, writing is a powerful way to find out what you think and feel. The act of writing by hand slows your thoughts giving time for you to hear and be taught by the Spirit of the Lord. In many ways, writing can be considered a form of meditation.

Some people find it more handy to use a computer to record their journal entries. They feel the protection of a personal password gives them an added layer of privacy. They also find it easier to look up and find past entries on particular topics.

One way or the other, typed or hand-written, your record of recovery is important. It will be a great help to you to process and come to realize your own truth and the truth that the Lord wants you to understand.

It is also good to have your journal to remind you of your journey and the details of the past. It is easy to get confused and overwhelmed by the deep sorrow and struggle you are wading through. A journal is a record of events and your response to them. It is a record of your intentions and your motives, your uncertainties and your decisions. As you record your prayerful thoughts and the Lord's personal counsel, it becomes a sacred record of His guidance to you as you sincerely try to receive it.

Praying and Pondering (Meditating)

Many of us have thought of prayer as an obligation or commandment, something that may have become as routine for us as brushing our teeth morning and night. As we face the crisis that addiction has presented us, we find ourselves unable to pray at all one day and the next day collapsed on the bed or the floor sobbing our hearts out to God. We have learned in recovery that this is one of the places where it helps so much to be assured of the mercy and patience of Heavenly

Father and the Savior. They understand. They are not going to abandon you because you are struggling to even want to pray.

Meditating, as it is practiced in Eastern religions where a person tries to empty his or her mind of all thought, is not the way meditation is taught in the Standard Works. In both the Old and New Testaments, as well as in the Doctrine and Covenants, meditation involves focusing our thoughts upon a scripture or upon the character of God Himself.[2] This same practice is also what is meant by "pondering."

Slow down. Muse upon a topic or idea. Use your imagination, guided by scripture and prayer, to be a receiving mechanism through which the Spirit of the Lord can communicate with you.

Fasting, Including Partial Fasts

Fasting magnifies the power of prayer. Fasting without prayer is nothing more than starving. Fasting is not a way of trying harder to get the Lord to do something. Fasting is an attempt to detach yourself from something that you consider essential in your life (usually food) so that you can give that time and attention to being in tune with the Spirit.

What you fast from doesn't always have to be food. We have learned that the spirit of fasting can be made effective in our lives by surrendering something the Lord is inviting us to let go of. For example, He may ask us to stop staying up too late and/or sleeping in too late. He may ask us to fast from overspending or escaping into media of one kind or another.

It is good to remember that the Lord accepts our efforts to fast from food, even when it is not every food. This was the example Daniel set for us when he refused to eat the meat and drink the wine the king supplied for him, requesting other more wholesome foods instead.[3]

The mention of fasting in the scriptures that has meant the most to both of us has been the account in which the Savior casts out the evil spirits that are causing a young man to do serious harm to himself.[4] The Lord's disciples had tried unsuccessfully to perform this act of healing. After Jesus accomplished it, they asked Him why they had failed. He answered them, **"This kind can come forth by nothing, but by prayer and fasting."**[5] We have found that addiction and codependency are definitely evils great enough to require the multiplied power of prayer and fasting combined.

Another Sister's Testimony of Her Own Recovery Program

After my husband got into recovery, I had to learn not to panic about the amount of time he spent attending recovery meetings and studying recovery principles. I also had to stop reading his literature and drilling him as to how he was doing and what he was learning. Instead, I had to get into recovery for myself so the Lord could teach me how to love my husband without needing to play the exhaustive role of his parent figure.

But I also experienced a sense of hope from being able to share my struggles and from knowing that others could understand. I learned that other people are making it through this darkness, and they have the desire to help others find their way as well. I don't want to exploit or relish in the struggles of my husband. I do however want to come to grips with how it has affected me, and what I need to do to protect myself spiritually.

I believe that we are pioneers in our own right—journeying through this vast dark and stormy desert, searching for truth and light and healing. Gratefully some have gone before us so that we can follow their path. But many more will sadly follow behind us. This is the place where we have come to finally and truly know God.

All I know is this: When I am working my program (prayer, scriptures, reading, meetings, writing, telephoning, and more prayer...) I can handle it. I am given gifts of understanding by the Spirit. I am comforted. I am even prompted to know the truth behind what he is saying to me—when he is not able to see anything but the lie.

I have also been given a witness by the Spirit of the love the Lord has for my husband. I know that He needs me to love him and allow him a safe place to heal. It is frightening to know that he may choose to not heal. But I know that regardless of his choice, I myself need to heal.   — *Jill*

Colleen: The Tools Magnified My Church Activity

I hadn't been in recovery too long when I began to see that just as there are external and internal tools of recovery, there are also external and internal tools of redemption. It is equally true that in the living of the gospel of Christ, there are activities that supply us with external support, such as attending our meetings, doing visiting and home teaching, and filling various callings.

In contrast, there are activities that no one sees us do, activities done in solitude just between us and the Lord, such as prayer, personal scripture study, and journaling. I neglected these internal activities for the first thirty years of my membership in the Church. I was so caught up in doing all the outward things a faithful, active Latter-day Saint should do that I felt justified in never getting around to the internal tools. I'm so grateful that through recovery I have learned to be active in the private places of my life and in my heart first. Internalization of these principles has magnified the blessings that I feel from being a member of the Lord's true Church.

1. The Nine Tools of Heart t' Heart is available as a PDF file at www.heart-t-heart.org

2. Joshua 1:8; Psalm 1:2; 77:12; 104:34; 119:15, 48, 78, 97, 99; 143:5; 1 Timothy 4:15; Doctrine & Covenants 76:19.

3. Daniel 1:8-16.

4. Mark 9:14-29.

5. Mark 9:29.

Chapter 18 *In Conclusion*

Well, if you've read through all the chapters of this book, it's a little like we've come to the end of a series of visits with you. Obviously, we haven't gotten to know you in the way we would have if we had really been able to sit down knee to knee and heart to heart in our living room or yours. Even so, we feel like we know you in a very special way because we can say without wavering that God has revealed to us His love for you. We can't picture you in our minds, but we can sense you reading these pages, even though it might be months or years after we wrote them. The Spirit of the Lord, after all, knows no time limits and brings all things into His presence at once—even the past, present, and future.[1] It might sound like we're talking fantasy or quantum physics or science fiction, but we're not. We're talking straight Mormon doctrine as we've lived it and learned to love it.

And so, with teary hugs and resolute smiles and sighs, we come to this concluding chapter. What more can we say? Sooner or later, we have to send our loved ones off on their own adventures. Between us, we've done that for seventeen children. We know what it feels like to have to hold our breath, chew our lip and watch them get in the car and drive away. We've learned how to let go and trust God—and trust them to God. And that's what we're going to do with each of you…in just a few more minutes.

But, first we have to say our personal good-byes.

Colleen: Learning to Trust the Love of a Good Man

My last prayer for you is that somehow in and through these hours of sharing, you have felt a glimmer of the truth that no matter what has happened with other men in your life (father, brothers, or husband) or what may still happen in the future—there is one good Man (well, actually three good Men) who will never fail you. Even though They cannot come to you physically at this time, I pray that you will seek to be spiritually-minded so that you can feel Their abiding presence in your heart and mind and in your home.

I pray, dear sister, that you will set your heart and mind to look to God and live through whatever your future may bring. I pray that you will seek the Holy Ghost with all your heart so that He can restore the premortal love and trust you had for your perfect Father in Heaven and your perfect Elder Brother. I testify to you with my whole soul that if you will turn to the Lord Jesus Christ, He will restore your faith in God, in yourself, in mankind, and recover for you the hope and enthusiasm with which you originally entered mortality.

Grounded in those recovered feelings of relationship to God, you will find yourself with less and less inclination to stay in or get back into a relationship with a man who would treat you unrighteously. Settle for nothing less than this standard: a man who has learned from the Lord, Himself, how to be a kind and gentle-hearted, gentle-handed, gentle-spirited man.

Turn to Christ. Let Him teach you how to love as only He can love. Remember that the greatest love you will ever feel for your husband will be the Lord's love for him. It is equally important that you know the greatest love you will ever receive in this life will not be your husband's, but the Lord's. This is the love that will sustain you, no matter who else in your life may fail you.

I remain ever your sister in this scary but amazing journey of mortality...

Phil: Just a Few Words of Goodbye...

This has been a wonderful experience, sharing our story with you and the hope we have in Christ. He has transformed my life and made it possible for my wife to have hope for the future. I recognize that my addiction could come back into active status again if I let my guard down, so I try to stay close to my Savior, who alone is responsible for the healing I have experienced.

In all honesty, though, I have to admit that this is not the solution I wanted at first. I wanted a guarantee, a complete release from this plague. The Lord has not seen fit to give me that. He has, however, given me peace and the knowledge that I can be clean and free from the clutches of the adversary by staying close to Him. At this writing, He has blessed me with more than ten years of abstinence from pornography. He has forgiven my past sins and given the comfort of His continued help. In short, He has given me Himself. What greater gift could a person ask?

While I still live in this telestial world filled with lures and temptations, I am exposed to the efforts of Satan to re-entrap me. I hope I am wiser than I used to be. Certainly I know how to find the strength from my Savior to repulse the temptations. At the same time, I see my sweet wife progressing in her own spiritual growth. I see the Lord leading her on and on, and it is beautiful to watch. So while total freedom from temptation seems to be delayed until mortality is over, what the Lord has given me so far is amazing. Colleen and I have a life together that is lived in Christ. He is the source we both turn to with our trials. He blesses us through each other. It is a marvelous three-way partnership.

As we come to the end of the book, I want to share with you an observation about my dear wife, Colleen. Perhaps you have noted this already yourself. It occurs to me that Colleen is the ideal person to write this book about wives dealing with sexually addicted husbands. She has dealt with two husbands with a sexual addiction, and with very different outcomes. Her first husband chose not to seek the path of honestly admitting his addiction and seeking recovery, and after years of struggle, Colleen was led to the decision that the marriage could not continue.

Divorce was the only option left to her. When Colleen married me, I was already attending Twelve Step meetings (Heart t' Heart). Although I still had a ways to go before I found lasting abstinence, she worked with me and shared with me what she had learned about recovery, and it blessed my life.

My point here is that Colleen had two very different experiences with two very different outcomes. The difference was not about her. I'm sure she would have been just as willing to work with her first husband had he chosen to follow that path. Her success with me was due to the fact that I wanted recovery and was willing to work the program. I hope that each of you can see that a good woman's efforts to support her husband in working through an addiction can be frustrated or rewarded by the husband's choices. It's an overwhelming testimony that whether your husband recovers or not is *not* about you. Choose to follow your own program of recovery and rebirth in Jesus Christ, and pray that your husband will choose to do the same.

We have shared our thoughts and a portion of our stories with you through this book, and while we haven't had the chance yet to hear your stories, I'm sure we someday will. Some of you will write to us and share them now. Others will share in a future beyond the veil. We already feel your spirits, and we rejoice and mourn with you, as needed. But the rejoicing will always triumph as we all follow our Lord and lay our burdens at His feet. This is our prayer for all of us.

1. Doctrine and Covenants 130:7.

You may write to Phil and Colleen
c/o Windhaven Publishing
PO Box 31
Hyrum, UT 84319

Appendix

What Is Capturing?

What does "capture" mean? It means to get hold of something, really get hold of it, and make it your own. Here's how you capture thoughts from any source.

1. If your source is in the form of written material, underline the words or phrases that stand out to you. If it's in the form of a lecture, take notes as you listen. (Remember, taking notes is not the same as taking dictation. The goal is not to recreate every word the speaker says. The goal is to note those single thoughts that stand out to you.)

    Most people think that this is the entire procedure, that this constitutes "capturing." Sorry. This is only the step of identifying what it is that you want to capture. (If you were an old-time cowboy and were sitting up on a ridge watching a herd of wild mustangs below you, just picking out the ones that look good to you is not the same as making them your own.)

2. Get a notebook of some sort (maybe a journal) and a pen and then rewrite the words, phrases, sentences or whatever you underlined or noted into that notebook. When I copy quotes, I usually underline them as well as put quote marks around them so they stand out from the rest of what I write.

    Now are you done? After all, you have written the thought down in your own notebook or journal. Sorry, this still does not make it your own. There is a third and final step. Without this last step you are only a collector of thoughts, not a captor.

3. Now write all that comes into your mind about the thought or quote that you have previously copied into your notebook. Why was it important to you? How did it connect for you? What does it say to you? How do you see that it applies to your life? This is capturing.

For me, this process of capturing thoughts, scriptures and quotes has also become a way of praying. I often find that I have just naturally entered into a prayer mode somewhere during this process, writing prayerful thoughts, expressing myself directly to God. And in just as easy and simple a manner I nearly always find myself realizing that what I am hearing in my thoughts is the voice of the Lord, through the Holy Spirit's mediation, speaking to my mind and heart (Colleen C. Harrison, *He Did Deliver Me from Bondage*, A–3, 4).

At first I resisted Colleen's suggestion about capturing. It just seemed like too much effort. After all, it was taking me long enough to get through the scriptures as it was. If I stopped and wrote about everything I read, I would never get through them! What an amazing new perspective hit me, though, when I realized that maybe "getting through" the scriptures might not be the most important way to approach them.

When at last I agreed to **"experiment upon [the] word" (Alma 32:27)** and try capturing for myself, I was amazed with the results. While I had experienced *occasional* new insights into the scriptures before, now I began to see new applications and meanings in virtually every verse I captured! I found as I *prayerfully* wrote down the thoughts and impressions that came into my mind, I could not deny that a Power greater than my own was inspiring and teaching me.

Years have passed since my first attempt to believe in the tool of capturing. I have used it almost daily to allow the Spirit of the Lord to guide my thoughts and my life. In fact, it was while I was capturing **Psalm 24:3–8** that I was led to the title of this book.

(Excerpted from *Clean Hands, Pure Heart* by Philip A. Harrison, Windhaven Publishing, 2004.)

The Twelve Steps
of Alcoholics Anonymous

1. We admitted we were powerless over alcohol—that our lives had become unmanageable.

2. Came to believe that a Power greater than ourselves could restore us to sanity.

3. Made a decision to turn our will and our lives over to the care of God as we understood Him.

4. Made a searching and fearless moral inventory of ourselves.

5. Admitted to God, to ourselves and to another human being the exact nature of our wrongs.

6. Were entirely ready to have God remove all these defects of character.

7. Humbly asked Him to remove our shortcomings.

8. Made a list of all persons we had harmed, and became willing to make amends to them all.

9. Made direct amends to such people wherever possible, except when to do so would injure them or others.

10. Continued to take personal inventory and when we were wrong promptly admitted it.

11. Sought through prayer and meditation to improve our conscious contact with God as we understood Him, praying only for knowledge of His will for us and the power to carry that out.

12. Having had a spiritual awakening as the result of these steps, we tried to carry this message to alcoholics, and to practice these principles in all our affairs.

The Twelve Steps of Heart t' Heart

1. **We admitted we were powerless over compulsive addictive behaviors*—that our lives had become unmanageable.** *Admitted that we of ourselves are powerless, nothing without God. (Mosiah 4:5; Alma 26:12)*

2. **Came to believe that a Power greater than ourselves could restore us to sanity.** *Came to believe that God has all power and all wisdom and that in His strength we can do all things. (Mosiah 4:9; Alma 26:12)*

3. **Made a decision to turn our will and our lives over to the care of God as we understood Him.** *Made the decision to reconcile ourselves to the will of God, offer our whole souls as an offering unto Him, and trust Him in all things forever. (2 Nephi 10:24; Omni 1:26; Mosiah 3:19; 2 Nephi 4:34)*

4. **Made a searching and fearless moral inventory of ourselves.** *Made a searching and fearless written inventory of our past in order to thoroughly examine ourselves as to our pride and other weaknesses with the intent of recognizing our own carnal state and our need for Christ's Atonement. (Alma 15:17; Mosiah 4:2; Jacob 4:6–7; Ether 12:27)*

5. **Admitted to God, to ourselves, and to another human being the exact nature of our wrongs.** *Honestly shared this inventory with God and with another person, thus demonstrating the sincerity of our repentance, and our willingness to give away all our sins that we might know Him. (Mosiah 26:29; Alma 22:18)*

6. **Were entirely ready to have God remove all these defects of character.** *Became humble enough to yield our hearts and our lives to Christ for His sanctification and purification, relying wholly upon His merits, acknowledging even our own best efforts as unprofitable. (Helaman 3:35; 2 Nephi 31:19; Mosiah 2:20–21)*

7. **Humbly asked Him to remove our shortcomings.** *Humbly cried unto the Lord Jesus Christ in our hearts for a remission of sins that through His mercy and His grace we might experience a mighty change of heart, lose all disposition to do evil, and thus be encircled about in the arms of safety because of His great and last sacrifice. (Alma 36:18; Alma 38:8; Moroni 10:32; Mosiah 5:2; Alma 34:15–16)*

8. **Made a list of all persons we had harmed and became willing to make amends to them all.** *Made a list of all persons we had harmed and became willing to make restitution to all of them (even those we had harmed in what we might have considered righteous anger), desiring instead to be peacemakers and to do all that we could to come unto God by being first reconciled to others. (3 Nephi 12:9; 3 Nephi 12:24; 3 Nephi 12:44–45)*

9. **Made direct amends to such people wherever possible except when to do so would injure them or others.** *Made restitution directly to those we had harmed, confessing our own wrongdoing in each instance except when to do so would further injure them or others. (Mosiah 27:35; 3 Nephi 12:25; Mosiah 26:30)*

10. **Continued to take personal inventory and when we were wrong promptly admitted it.** *Realizing that the weakness to be tempted and to sin is a part of the mortal experience, we continued to take personal inventory and when we were wrong promptly admitted it, being willing to repent as often as needed. (2 Nephi 4:18; 2 Nephi 10:20; Mosiah 26:30)*

11. **Sought through prayer and meditation to improve our conscious contact with God as we understood Him, praying only for knowledge of His will for us and the power to carry that out.** *Sought through prayer and meditation to improve our conscious contact with God, seeking the words of Christ through the power of the Holy Ghost that they might tell us all things that we should do, praying only for a knowledge of His will for us and the power to carry that out. (2 Nephi 32:3; Alma 37:37; Helaman 10:4)*

12. **Having had a spiritual awakening as the result of these steps, we tried to carry this message to others still suffering from the effects of compulsive behaviors and to practice these principles in all our affairs.** *Having experienced a mighty change and having awakened unto God as a result of our sincere repentance demonstrated in taking these steps, we were willing to become instruments in carrying this message to others and to practice these principles in all our affairs. (Alma 5:7; Mosiah 27:36–37; Moroni 7:3)*

*Any problem may be inserted here, in place of "compulsive addictive behaviors."

Permission to use the Twelve Steps of Alcoholics Anonymous for adaptation granted by A.A. World Services, Inc.

Excerpted from the pamphlet, "The Twelve Steps of Heart t' Heart." Reprinted with permission from Heart t' Heart General Service Board.

What If a Criminal Act Has Been Committed?

It is horrifying to realize the depths of sin into which Satan can drag an addicted person. It is truly awful to realize that a person can become so infected and deluded by Satan's lies that they can end up committing acts of evil they would have shrunk from in horror only a few short years before.

We would like to hope and pray that the Saints could be immune to Satan's powers, but obviously we are not. Being members of the Lord's restored Church does not equate with us being any less mortal than our brothers and sisters throughout the world. We can be sure that the adversary's intentions towards the LDS people today are just as desirous of our destruction as they were toward the Nephites when the Savior warned the people gathered at Bountiful that Satan desired to **"sift** [them] **as wheat."**[1]

What you as a wife must not do is allow your conscience to become so seared and numb to these influences that you ignore or excuse actions your husband is doing in the privacy of your home that may be getting close to or have possibly already crossed the line into criminal behavior. If you suspect that your husband may be engaged in illegal behaviors—especially those that involve children or child pornography—we hope you will respond calmly but firmly in following up on your suspicion to ensure the safety of yourself and your children. It is also important for you to remember that it is possible for you to be held accountable for any illegal actions you have knowledge of but do not report to proper authorities.

In the following pages we will be addressing only three forms of behavior that could either precipitate illegal behaviors or have already become. We are aware that there are as many different variations on these illegal behaviors as there are case histories to be considered. Still, we would like to offer some thoughts that might bolster your courage to examine the possibility that your experience may be sliding into this degree of tragic possibility. You must realize that you may be the instrument the Lord needs to rescue yourself and your children.

Here are three categories of behaviors that are considered criminal offenses in most of the developed nations of the world.

Domestic Violence

When most of us hear the phrase, "domestic violence," we picture physical force and obvious injuries. The sad reality is that there are many non-physical ways that a man could be abusing his wife without anyone outside their home being aware of it. He may be calling her rude and disrespectful names, criticizing and belittling her, humiliating her, making her feel worthless, ugly, stupid, or crazy, or frequently using sarcasm against her. He may also be very dominating and controlling of her access to outside friendships and activities, as well as not allowing her to spend any money without his consent. He may threaten her with physical harm and do just enough grabbing and pushing to keep her afraid of him.

Even though these behaviors do not qualify as "criminal," years of exposure to them can take a terrible toll on a wife and other family members. She may develop such symptoms as chronic fear, nightmares, sleep disturbance, anxiety, anger, difficulty concentrating, depression, low self-esteem, shame and embarrassment, chronic physical complaints, substance abuse, eating disorders (anorexia or compulsive overeating), social withdrawal, feelings of helplessness and hopelessness, self-blame, self-abuse, emotional numbness on one hand and hypervigilence (inability to relax) on the other. She may take upon herself the blame for her reactions, believing, as her husband will often accuse her, that she is making them up. Furthermore, becoming conditioned to these abuses may set her up for later physical abuse, which is a criminal act.

An even sadder repercussion of this type of abuse in marriage is that children growing up in such an environment are almost certainly developing many of these behavior patterns themselves. Tragically, they represent yet another generation that is going to be deeply affected and powerfully predisposed to become either domestic abusers or victims themselves.

Unfortunately, these forms of emotional and verbal abuse occur in far too many LDS homes under the guise of a husband's perverted excuse that he holds some sort of authority over his wife and children. We hope that if you are living with the kind of circumstances described above that you will prayerfully read the following verse from the Doctrine and Covenants as often as you need in order *to know beyond a doubt* that you have absolutely no religious or spiritual obligation to respect your husband's priesthood when he behaves in such a manner. As this verse so plainly states, he has none.

> **That** [the priesthood] **may be conferred upon** [men]**, it is true; but when we undertake to cover our sins, or to gratify our pride, our vain ambition,** *or to exercise control or dominion or compulsion upon the souls of the children of men, in any degree of unrighteousness,* **behold, the heavens withdraw themselves; the Spirit of the Lord is grieved; and when it is withdrawn,** *Amen to the priesthood or the authority of that man* **(Doctrine & Covenants 121:37, emphasis added).**

Another reason to take these non-physical forms of abuse seriously, especially if you feel their frequency or intensity escalating, is that they can be early warning signs that your husband is spiraling further down into a state of emotional and spiritual dishonesty and darkness that may eventually explode into acts of physical violence.

Domestic violence, ultimately, can take the inexcusable form of spousal battering. We wish we could say that there are no LDS homes where this sorrow occurs, but we cannot. It is so important that you not let shame or embarrassment stop you from going to the authorities for help, even if you have been guilty of initiating these violent episodes yourself. When the dysfunction in a marriage has reached the stage of physical violence, there is virtually no hope of it ceasing without professional and perhaps legal intervention.

According to the United States Department of Justice, in the United States 4 out of every 5 victims of spousal violence in 2005 were women, and 4 out of 5 of all people killed by their spouses were women.[2] In light of this major difference in the ratio of battered and murdered wives to husbands, it becomes imperative for you to get help as soon as possible.

Sexual Abuse of a Spouse Within Marriage

Sexual abuse of a spouse qualifies as a form of domestic violence, but we felt it important to consider it separately since we are addressing the wife of a sexually addicted man. Only in the last several decades has the idea emerged that a man's sexual demands on his wife could be classified as abuse or rape. In the past, the legal position in most of the United States was that when a woman married a man, she was automatically giving consent to be involved or used by him in any sexual way he required of her, whether she consented to the act on any particular occasion or not. Fortunately, this barbaric underestimation of a woman's worth and her role as a wife has no place in the gospel of Christ or in His restored Church. We are so grateful that laws reflecting more respect for married women are being instituted in society.

There are many websites on the Internet where you can find further information on this issue. We pray you will take advantage of these resources if you find yourself feeling forced into sexual actions with which you are not in wholehearted agreement. This is especially true if the forced act is one of intercourse, or marital rape. It is a terrible oversight even to this day that most people (including the perpetrators and the victims) do not realize that marital rape can in some ways be even more damaging psychologically and spiritually than stranger rape because it destroys the trust that is the basic requirement of a genuine marriage.

Your husband *does not* have the right to dominate you in this area of life—not in the eyes of the law, or of the Church, or of God.

Child Sexual Abuse

Perhaps the most heinous sexual crimes imaginable are those perpetrated against children by their own parents. Such actions shock and outrage most people because they are a violation of a very basic instinct in healthy parents—to protect their children, even at the cost of their own lives. And yet, some men (and sadly, even some women) get drawn into the horrifying lie that they have the right to be sexual with their children.

If you discover your husband is involved in a transgression of this magnitude, we pray that you will immediately alert the proper authorities so that your husband and your child, as well as yourself, can be rescued and set on a path toward recovery as soon as possible. Your bishop, branch president or stake president may be one of the first sources of help to which you can appeal. In recent years, the Church has been training local priesthood leaders more thoroughly on what to do in these types of situations. Your ecclesiastical leader should be prepared with the information you need to help you contact the law enforcement authorities and to find agencies that specialize in providing rescue and counseling for you and your child.

It is especially important that your child receive the best counseling you can arrange, preferably with a counselor who specializes in child psychology. If a child has been victimized, that child needs to hear the truth spoken plainly and repeatedly from as many adults as possible that the abuse *was not* his or her fault. This is vital, because close family members who molest children will often manipulate the child into believing that he or she invited the abuse.

In addition, a young child is not psychologically mature enough to comprehend that their father, who the child all but worships, could be the one doing wrong. Thus, the statements of the courts and other authorities in making the offender responsible for his actions can help the child eventually recover from feeling guilty.

While it is true that the consequences of disclosing child sexual abuse in your home will most likely bring about extreme disruption of your family circumstances, the alternative of keeping such activity secret is unconscionable. To keep such a thing secret in order to spare your reputation in your community, or even for your own personal safety or comfort, is the moral equivalent of being an accomplice in exactly the kind of offense the Savior described in some of the harshest words He ever uttered.

> **Then said he unto the disciples, It is impossible but that offences will come: but woe unto him, through whom they come! It were better for him that a millstone were hanged about his neck, and he cast into the sea, than that he should offend one of these little ones (Luke 17:1-2).**

If you are the parent who has the agonizing task of reporting the abuse, remember that whatever the consequences or repercussions may be, *they are not your fault.* You must cling tightly to this truth, because you can be almost certain that your husband will blame you.

You must never forget that by the time a person has descended to such depths of degradation as to sexually abuse a child, they are usually quick to blame anyone, including you and the child, for their piteous situation. You must support and defend your child against such lies, especially if he or she first disclosed the abuse. Never lose sight of the truth that the person who broke the law carries the *entire* weight of responsibility for the results of his actions.

Another aspect of the child's healing is spiritual. Please do not let anyone under any circumstances suggest that the child needs to repent. He or she has *not* sinned, even if they may have experienced sexual arousal during the abuse. Help him or her to know that Heavenly Father and the Savior are both loving and kind, and that part of what Jesus suffered for in the Garden of Gethsemane was the pains and sorrows we would experience in this life as the result of other people's sins.

Phil: A Disturbing Letter

I will never forget a letter I received from a mother whose husband had involved their teenage daughter in sexual contact. The mother was afraid to report what she knew to the authorities because of the risk to her husband's job and to his reputation in the community. The mother talked to her daughter who reassured her that she was "all right." Greatly relieved to hear her daughter define the incident in such a trivialized way, the mother concluded that the girl needed no further intervention. In reality, the daughter had told her mother what she knew her mother wanted to hear. Thus, nothing was disclosed to anyone outside the home because (to use the mother's words) to do so would "ruin everything."

The response in my own heart and mind was immediate shock and sorrow. I have read widely enough on these issues to know that a young girl who has been sexually molested by her own father—even if it is only once—is far from being "all right" emotionally and psychologically. Let me suggest a metaphor for this situation. Picture that while going barefoot in the yard, she has stepped on a board with a rusty nail in it. Her parents remove the nail, but they do not call the doctor or check her immunizations because, after all, there was hardly any blood and she said she was "all right." Was the girl truly injured? Was the injury going to get worse? Of course it was!

I wrote back to the mother and emphasized to her that her daughter was not all right. I have no idea what course the woman followed, but I could not help wondering what damage had been done to their daughter. What repercussions would continue to unfold from her knowing that her father was capable of feeling and acting upon lust toward her? Even though she said she was "all right," how would such a situation affect her sense of safety in her home and in her future interactions with her father?

The secrecy practiced by the parents in this story would undoubtedly delay the healing in their daughter, but what would it also do to the possibility of healing in the father? Hiding a sin not only postpones the healing process, it allows the infection of evil in a person's soul to spread and intensify. While the consequences of this degree of wrongdoing are great, they must be faced if the perpetrator is to repent, and if both the victim and the perpetrator are to heal.

For more information on legal issues particularly relating to pornography, see the chapter "Pornography and the Law: Legal Issues for Clergy, Counselors, and Others" by Merrill F. Nelson, pp 217-229 in *Confronting Pornography* edited by Chamberlain, Gray and Reid (see appendix).

1. 3 Nephi 18:18.

2. Matthew R. Durose et al., U.S. Dep't of Just., NCJ 207846, Bureau of Justice Statistics, Family Violence Statistics: Including Statistics on Strangers and Acquaintances, at 31-32 (2005), available at http://www.ojp.usdoj.gov/bjs/pub/pdf/fvs.pdf

Resources for Recovery

Organizations and Websites for Addicts and Loved Ones

While this list is by no means exhaustive, it contains some of the organizations we are familiar with that deal with addiction and the challenges faced by the addicts' loved ones. You can easily find many more organizations through a simple Internet search. We have tried to list those sites and fellowships that we have found to be most compatible with the values of the LDS Church.

LDS Sponsored or Oriented Organizations

LDS Family Services Addiction Recovery Program (ARP)
www.providentliving.org/content/list/0,11664,4177-1,00.html
From this home page for the ARP program, you can look up locations of local face-to-face meetings. You can also download the ARP Guide: *A Guide to Addiction Recovery and Healing,* as a PDF or as an audio file.

About their meetings, Family Services says: "LDS Family Services sponsors addiction recovery support meetings to assist individuals who desire freedom from addiction and a better life through gospel fellowship. These meetings are ongoing, free, and confidential. Meetings typically last between 60 and 90 minutes. Experienced group leaders create a safe environment where participants can encourage one another and implement gospel principles in their efforts to recover and heal."

LDS Family Services Pornography Addiction Support Groups (PASG)
There is not a separate website for the PASG meetings. Times and places are included in the ARP schedule listed above. In many places meetings are held for both the addict and the spouse, usually at the same time but in different rooms at the same location.

Heart t' Heart
www.heart-t-heart.org

Heart t' Heart is an LDS-oriented Twelve Step/Twelve Tradition organization that supports the teaching and doctrines of the Church. Help is offered through face-to-face and online meetings, forums, literature and audio recordings.

Windhaven Publishing
www.windhavenpublishing.com

Windhaven Publishing/Windhaven Recovery is the self-publishing and recovery support effort of Colleen and Phil Harrison and is responsible for the book you are reading. Other LDS Twelve Step recovery books are available through Windhaven Publishing, such as *He Did Deliver Me from Bondage* and *Clean Hands, Pure Heart,* as well as audio recordings and artwork. A forum for discussion of recovery issues and literature is also available on the website.

Online LDS-Oriented Websites

Combating Pornography
http://combatingpornography.org

Sponsored by LDS Family Services, this site includes references to other resources, including talks by LDS General Authorities. The website states: "If you or someone you love is struggling with pornography, there is hope. We have articles and resources for five audiences: individuals, parents, spouses, youth and leaders."

Mormon Mommy Blogs
http://mormonmommyblogs.blogspot.com

This site features blogs by LDS women on various topics. Enter "pornography" in the search box to find posts relative to this issue. You can read what other LDS women have said about their experiences as loved ones of pornography addicts.

LDS Addiction Recovery
www.ldsar.org

This site includes blogs for addicts and codependents. Their mission statement says: "LDS Addiction Recovery was founded with the goal of helping addicts recover through writing. Writing is very important for addicts and their loved ones, as it can assist us in sorting through our feelings and healing emotionally. LDS Addiction Recovery seeks to provide a safe environment for addicts and loved ones to be able to share and, through sharing, assist others as well."

Latter-Day Sexual Recovery
www.ldsr.org

This site contains much information, including blogs and forums for those who struggle with sexual addictions; spouses of those who struggle with sexual addictions; those who struggle with body image issues; and those who struggle with same-sex attraction.

Non-LDS Organizations

Some of the following organizations are oriented toward the addict, but many have a companion organization for family members and other loved ones. We recommend looking into these organizations, both for personal help and support and also for a greater understanding of addiction in general. We find it doesn't matter what one's challenge is—the literature of one organization is easily understood by individuals suffering with a different challenge. For example, literature for the wives of alcoholics is very useful to wives of sex addicts.

S-Anon
www.sanon.org

"S-Anon is a program of recovery for those who have been affected by someone else's sexual behavior. S-Anon is based on the Twelve Steps and the Twelve Traditions of Alcoholics Anonymous."

Sexaholics Anonymous
www.sa.org

"Sexaholics Anonymous is a fellowship of men and women who share their experience, strength, and hope with each other that they may solve their common problem and help others to recover. The only requirement for membership is a desire to stop lusting and become sexually sober. Our primary purpose is to stay sexually sober and help others to achieve sexual sobriety."

Co-Dependents Anonymous
www.coda.org

We have discussed the phenomenon of codependency in Chapters Eight and Nine. CoDA is devoted to helping people dealing with any type of codependent relationship. They describe themselves in these words: "CoDA is a fellowship of men and women whose common purpose is to develop healthy relationships. The only requirement for membership is a desire for healthy and loving relationships."

Al-Anon/Alateen
www.al-anon.org

"For over 55 years, Al-Anon (which includes Alateen for younger members) has been offering strength and hope for friends and families of problem drinkers. It is estimated that each alcoholic affects the lives of at least four other people…alcoholism is truly a family disease. No matter what relationship you have with an alcoholic, whether they are still drinking or not, all who have been affected by someone else's drinking can find solutions that lead to serenity in the Al-Anon/Alateen fellowship."

Alcoholics Anonymous
www.aa.org

AA is the "parent" organization of all other Twelve Step fellowships, having first expounded the principles we know as the Twelve Steps in the 1930s. They describe themselves this way: "Alcoholics Anonymous® is a fellowship of men and women who share their experience, strength and hope with each other that they may solve their common problem and help others to recover from alcoholism. The only requirement for membership is a desire to stop drinking. AA is not allied with any sect, denomination, politics, organization or institution; does not wish to engage in any controversy, neither endorses nor opposes any causes. Our primary purpose is to stay sober and help other alcoholics to achieve sobriety."

Miracles In Progress 12 Step Recovery
http://www.12stepforums.net

"Miracles In Progress 12 Step Recovery" is a clearing house with information gathered from a number of Twelve Step organizations, such as Alcoholics Anonymous (AA), Al-Anon Family Group, Adult Children Anonymous (ACA), Narcotics Anonymous (NA), and Childhood Abuse Survivors (CAS). The Miracles website gives links to forums and online Twelve Step meetings and general Twelve Step support chat.

Recommended Books for Recovery

LDS-Oriented Books

He Did Deliver Me from Bondage by Colleen C. Harrison, Revised Edition, Windhaven Publishing, 1991-2002.

This is the original book that laid the foundation for the LDS Twelve Step recovery movement. It is still considered the primer for studying the steps and using them to access the principles of repentance and recovery through the Atonement of Jesus Christ.

Clean Hands, Pure Heart: Overcome Addiction to Pornography through the Redeeming Power of Jesus Christ by Philip A. Harrison, Windhaven Publishing, 2004.

After being in recovery and having several years of solid abstinence from his own addiction to pornography, Phil felt the Lord call him to lay his reputation on the line and offer his voice of lived experience to help other LDS men caught in the trap of sexual addiction. Includes study questions for each step.

Dear Bishop by Philip A. Harrison. Windhaven Publishing, 2005.

Phil wrote this booklet based on the things that he wished his priesthood leaders had understood about addiction during the interviews he had with them over the years as he struggled to find lasting abstinence. Phil felt that one way he could help bishops and others seeking to help addicts was to share the benefit of his own experience.

Patterns of Light by Colleen C. Harrison. Windhaven Publishing, 2000-2005.

This series of booklets on each of the Twelve Steps (currently available through Step Six), relates them to passages from the Book of Mormon and original literature of Alcoholics Anonymous. These are an excellent resource for someone who has worked through *He Did Deliver Me from Bondage* and would like to continue their scripture-guided study of the Twelve Steps.

A Voice from the Fire: The Authority of Experience by Colleen C. Harrison. Windhaven Publishing, 2002.

An inside look at Colleen's personal struggle to find the Lord in her own journey and to find His will for her after sexual addiction destroyed her first marriage. It is a collection of short personal essays and memoir chapters, alternating with poems in which she expresses her feelings at key moments in her recovery.

Addiction Recovery Program: A Guide to Addiction Recovery and Healing. LDS Family Services, 2005.

The official study guide for both the LDS Family Services Addiction Recovery Program (ARP) and also for the LDS Family Services Pornography Addiction Support Groups (PASG). It offers a brief overview of each step and what a person needs to do to return to activity in the church (assuming they have become less active due to their addiction). It also provides scripture-guided study and writing exercises for each step. The entire text of this book can be found at the Provident Living website listed above or at LDS Church Distribution.

Confronting Pornography edited by Mark D. Chamberlain, Daniel D. Gray and Rory C. Reid. Deseret Book, 2005.

Each chapter in this book is written by a different author and gives the reader a comprehensive overview of the subject of pornography addiction from a variety of perspectives ranging from the addict and his loved ones to professional counselors and researchers in the addiction field. Phil and Colleen Harrison were grateful to be able to contribute chapters to this book based on their own life experiences in recovery.

The Worth of Every Soul by Gerald Curtis (Steven A. Cramer) and LoAnn Curtis. Cedar Fort, 2004.

Gerald and LoAnn share their story of Gerald's sexual addiction which led to excommunication from the Church, followed by, as he puts it, "conversion" and rebaptism. Gerald explains how the love of the Savior brought him back. Gerald has also published several other excellent books under his pen name Steven A. Cramer.

Willpower is Not Enough: Why We don't Succeed at Change by A. Dean Byrd and Mark D. Chamberlain. Deseret Book, 1995.
Everyone who has struggled with addiction knows the heartache of trying to stop the addictive behavior. Byrd and Chamberlain help us to understand the need for a power greater than ourselves.

Hold on to Hope: Help for LDS Addicts and Their Families complied by Hidden Treasures Institute, with contributions by Vaughn J. Featherstone and Dr. Rick H. Cedar Fort, Inc., 1996.

This book contains explanations of addiction from both professional and gospel points of view, plus stories of addicts themselves and family members who have been impacted by the addictions of their loved ones.

Understanding & Healing Codependency with Gospel Principles by
John C. Turpin. Covenant Communications, Inc, 1992.

Dr. Turpin illustrates the most common symptoms and results of
codependency and gives clear guidelines for using gospel principles to
chart progress. He sorts out the confusing differences between codependent service and true Christ-like service.

Some Valuable Non-LDS Books

A Codependent's Guide to the Twelve Steps by Melody Beattie.
Prentice Hall, 1990.

Melody Beattie is one of the pioneers in writing about codependency. This guide was the original text used by Co-Dependents
Anonymous. Beattie has a wonderful, readable style and this book is
filled with powerful insights about on applying the Twelve Steps to codependency.

Codependent No More by Melody Beattie. Harper & Row/Hazelden, 1987.

One of the first books to bring the concept of codependency to the
general public. Beattie's very readable style combined with her experience both as a codependent herself and as a professional counselor
make her series of books on codependency very valuable reading.

Co-Dependents Anonymous. Co-Dependents Anonymous, 1995.

The official text of the Twelve Step organization CoDA listed above.

S-Anon: Twelve Steps. S-Anon International Family Groups, 2000.

S-Anon is the companion organization to SA that helps the family
and friends of sexually addicted loved ones adapt and apply the Twelve
Steps to their own journey of recovery. Filled with first-person stories
and testimonies of recovery by other women as they use each step.

Sexaholics Anonymous. SA Literature, 1989-2002

The "SA White Book" is one of the best books you can read to
understand sexual addiction. The presentation is personal and rigor-

ously honest. Phil found this book extremely helpful in his own recovery.

Living with an Alcoholic with the Help of Al-Anon. Al-Anon Family Group, 1976.

A good book for loved ones of addicts of any kind. The principles are the same no matter how the addict is "acting out".

Al-Anon's Twelve Steps & Twelve Traditions. Al-Anon Family Group, 1990.

The basic text of Al-Anon with personal stories to illustrate application of the steps and traditions in the lives of loved ones of addicts.

Alcoholics Anonymous (The A.A. "Big Book"). A.A. World Services, Inc. Fourth Edition, 1939-2001.

The "AA Big Book" is the foundation of all other Twelve Step literature and programs. Many who do not struggle with alcoholism are amazed to find how broadly and easily the principles in this book apply to them and their own need to grow and change.

**Recovery books from Windhaven Publishing may be purchased through most LDS bookstores or at www.windhavenpublishing.com, the Windhaven Publishing. Sample chapters are available for download at the website and some titles are available in audio, e-book and/or pdf formatting.

INDEX

—Quote Index—

—NOTES—

—NOTES—

ABOUT THE AUTHOR

Colleen C. Harrison, mother of twelve children, has survived the death of her oldest daughter and the loss of her first marriage to addictive behavior. Drawing on the power (grace) of Jesus Christ and her own life experiences, Colleen has merged gospel teachings, psychology, human development and creative writing to create a uniquely LDS version of narrative therapy.

Founder of Heart t' Heart, an LDS Twelve Step community resource, Colleen holds a BA and MA in English from Brigham Young University, has completed training for certification as an Addictions Counselor from the University of Utah, and has finished all of the course work for a PhD in Family and Human Development from Utah State University. She has since retired from degree seeking status to better enjoy the blessing of "a marriage literally made in heaven" and to concentrate her energies on writing and developing Windhaven Recovery, Inc. (WRI).

Colleen is the author of *He Did Deliver Me from Bondage*, the LDS Twelve Step study guide that was used by LDS Family Services for ten years during the "pilot program" phase of their Addiction Recovery Program. She served on the committee of recovering LDS addicts that created the original draft of the current LDS Family Services study guide. She is also the author of *A Voice From the Fire: The Authority of Experience*, a memoir based on her life's experiences as the mother in an active LDS family that was eventually overwhelmed and destroyed by hidden addictions. She has been a presenter at Brigham Young University Education Weeks, both in Idaho and Utah, and has spoken at many conferences throughout the United States and Canada.

Philip A. Harrison is a life-long member of The Church of Jesus Christ of Latter-day Saints, born and raised in Provo, Utah. He served a mission to Germany. In keeping with family academic traditions, Phil graduated from BYU with bachelor's and master's degrees in botany, then from the University of Georgia in Athens with a Ph.D., also in botany, with an emphasis in plant physiology. He worked for twenty-five years as a plant physiologist for the USDA, most of that time in Logan Utah. He retired in January, 2010, to devote more time to helping the addiction recovery movement in the LDS community.

Phil was married to Kathy Francis for almost twenty-nine years before she passed away from heart disease. They are the parents of five children. Following graduate school, Phil and Kathy lived in upstate New York and California before returning to Utah, where for fifteen years they led workshops in the "Inner Peace Through Self-Mastery" program (an LDS-oriented adaptation of Recovery Inc., a cognitive therapy approach to emotional health). Kathy had twenty-five years of experience in Twelve Step work, and passed away only five months after discovering the LDS-oriented Twelve Step program, Heart t' Heart. Following Kathy's passing, Phil married Colleen. He is the author of *Clean Hands, Pure Heart: Overcoming Addiction to Pornography Through the Redeeming Power of Jesus Christ.*

Colleen and Phil live "after the manner of happiness" in a cheerful, peaceful home which sees a continual stream of family (they have a combined total of seventeen children and a growing number of grand-children) and friends. Both Colleen and Phil are active authors who devote their lives to carrying the message of sanity, security, and remission of sin through the principles of recovery expressed in these pages.

You may write to Colleen or Phil c/o Windhaven Publishing and Productions, P.O. Box 31, Hyrum, UT 84319

"WE CARE" LIST

Using the telephone or e-mail to contact others is a means of breaking through our isolation and getting back on the road to recovery. It has been compared to having a meeting between meetings. I encourage you to use this page to begin building a personal phone list that you can use to reach out to others.

Name	Phone	E-mail

Order Form

To order additional copies of *From Heartache to Healing* and other Windhaven products, send this order form along with check or money order in US dollars to:

Windhaven Publishing, P.O. Box 31, Hyrum, UT 84319

OR order online at www.windhavenpublishing.com

ITEM	PRICE	X	QTY.	=	TOTAL
From Heartache to Healing, Colleen C. & Philip A. Harrison	$16.95*	X	_____	=	_____
Clean Hands, Pure Heart, Philip A. Harrison	$17.95*	X	_____	=	_____
He Did Deliver Me from Bondage, Colleen C. Harrison	$14.95*	X	_____	=	_____
A Voice from the Fire, Colleen C. Harrison	$11.95*	X	_____	=	_____
Patterns of Light: Step 1, Colleen C. Harrison	$3.50*	X	_____	=	_____
Patterns of Light: Step 2, Colleen C. Harrison	$3.50*	X	_____	=	_____
Patterns of Light: Step 3, Colleen C. Harrison	$3.50*	X	_____	=	_____
Patterns of Light: Steps 4&5, Colleen C. Harrison	$3.50*	X	_____	=	_____
Patterns of Light: Step 6, Colleen C. Harrison	$3.50*	X	_____	=	_____
Dear Bishop, Colleen C. Harrison	$1.95*	X	_____	=	_____

Subtotal _____

Sales Tax: Add 6.6% for books shipped to Utah address _____

Shipping: 15% of Subtotal, minimum $3.00 in U.S. only
Canada/Overseas, call for rates. _____

Total Enclosed _____

Please Print:

Date: _____ Phone: (_____)_____

Name: _____

Address: _____

City, ST, ZIP _____

Copy this page as needed for orders. If Ship-To address is different than above, please note on back. Credit card orders may be placed online at www.windhavenpublishing.com or by phone at 877.245.4786 or by fax at 435.245.3723

* Prices subject to change without notice.